TEMPLE *of* T
and Other Inc
of Indian Monuments

Storytrails, an organization that showcases India through her stories, is a pioneer in designing unique, story-based walking tours, audio tours and local experiences across India. Since 2007, Storytrails has taken its story-based learning programmes to many schools across India. Its YouTube channel, 'Three Minute Storytrails', explores fascinating stories of people, places and monuments of India in bite-sized videos. Storytrails is a winner of the 'Creative Entrepreneurship Award' from the British Council, and the 'Travellers' Choice' and 'Hall of Fame' awards from Tripadvisor, among others. The Storytrails team is a group of experienced writers, researchers and storytellers from diverse backgrounds who share a passion for history.

Know more about Storytrails at www.storytrails.in

The
TEMPLE *of* TREASURES
and Other Incredible Tales
of Indian Monuments

Storytrails

First published in 2022 by Hachette India
(Registered name: Hachette Book Publishing India Pvt. Ltd)
An Hachette UK company
www.hachetteindia.com

1

Contributors for the stories in this book are:
Research and writing: Akila Raman, Kaushik S.V., Nayantara Nayar and Vijay Prabhat
Kamalakara; Proofreading and editing: Divya Subramaniam and Jayashree Menon.

ISBN 978-93-91028-17-6

Hachette Book Publishing India Pvt. Ltd
4th & 5th Floors, Corporate Centre
Plot No. 94, Sector 44, Gurugram – 122003, India

Typeset in Bembo Std 12/15.8
by Manmohan Kumar, Delhi

Printed and bound in India
by Manipal Technologies Limited, Manipal

Contents

I

Decoding the Brahmi Script

FEROZ SHAH KOTLA, DELHI

Two thousand years ago there lived a wise king
Who left his word on pillars and stones;
People over time wondered at them in passing,
As to them this ancient script was unknown.
What secrets did these squiggles hide?
It took an Englishman to find
The name of the king who took far and wide
The teachings of a religion that soon declined.

Inscription in Brahmi on the pillar of Sarnath

Which is the oldest script in India? We don't have a definite answer to that, but one of the oldest *readable* scripts of South and Central Asia is called the Brahmi script. It used to be called the stick-figure script, because all the letters looked like stick figures. In fact, for over a thousand years, the script was completely indecipherable to us. No one could read it or make sense of it. Today, we can. So how was this ancient script decoded?

Two thousand years ago, there lived a great king who ruled almost all of India. This powerful king was a devotee of the Buddha. He very wisely inscribed all his ideas, laws and commands on rock faces and pillars. Then he put them up across the Indian subcontinent. He wanted generations of people to read his words. His idea worked. For many years, passers-by read these inscriptions and praised this great king and his many brilliant ideas.

Time went on. Gradually, new scripts came up, and became popular. People stopped writing in the ancient script that this great king had used, and they forgot about his inscriptions too.

Cut to a thousand years later. In the 1350s, Delhi was ruled by a king named Feroz Shah Tughlaq. One day he was out hunting in the forest, when he spotted a beautiful pillar with some strange inscriptions on it. No one knew what it said or who put it there. But Feroz Shah thought it would make an elegant decoration for his new capital city, Feroz Shah Kotla (in modern-day Delhi). He carted the pillar back with him and had it installed at his citadel. Nearly 700 years later, you can still see the pillar standing stoically at Feroz Shah Kotla.

Around 236–237 BCE, Ashoka had commissioned several pillars on which his commands were inscribed. Most of these inscriptions contain only six edicts about right conduct in his kingdom. But the pillar that King Feroz Shah Tughlaq installed at his fort is special for a reason. This contains a rare seventh edict that explains what Ashoka did for upholding morality and why. This is one of the two Ashokan pillars in Delhi. The other one stands outside the Bara Hindu Rao Hospital.

Now let's jump forward to the 1800s, when the British controlled India. Some of the Englishmen were fascinated by Indian history. In those days, people knew very little about the country's ancient history. One of the main reasons for this was that no one could read ancient inscriptions like the ones on Feroz Shah's pillar. Strangely enough, the script that appeared on it wasn't seen just on that one pillar. British archaeologists found the same script scattered across India – on pillars and rocks.

At that time, there was an Englishman named James Prinsep, who was an employee of the British East India Company. He was a metallurgist at the East India Company's mint. But Prinsep was not an ordinary metallurgist; he dabbled in many subjects like astronomy, architecture, metrology, meteorology, history, drawing and linguistics. He enjoyed studying old coins. This led him to another field of study. Over time, he noticed that many of the old coins from around India had a variety of scripts inscribed on them. So he taught himself to become an epigraphist or a scholar of ancient scripts.

James Prinsep was an expert in many other fields as well – rocks, fossils, map-making and architecture, among others. Prinsep was also a talented artist. He was the founding editor of the *Journal of the Asiatic Society of Bengal*. Unfortunately, he died when he was just forty, so the world lost a gifted Indologist all too soon.

When Prinsep spotted Feroz Shah's pillar, he was intrigued. What did it say? What mysterious secrets did these inscriptions hide? Nobody knew, but Prinsep had a hunch. He learnt that a Norwegian Indologist, Christian Lassen, had done pioneering work on bilingual inscriptions. When an inscription had the same matter written in two different languages, it was possible to decipher the unknown language using the known language as the base. Lassen's research gave Prinsep a foundation to work on, and he decided to take Lassen's approach further. Many of the coins he was studying had Greek markings on one side and inscriptions in ancient Indian scripts on the other side. Prinsep was adept at reading ancient Greek. Using that knowledge, he began interpreting the other side. Some letters and syllables began to make sense. Slowly, he began to notice a pattern: one word kept appearing in many of these inscriptions. That word was *daanam*, meaning 'donation'. Prinsep began to realize that the inscriptions were about a king

Feroz Shah Kotla Pillar

What's the difference between a language and a script?
A script refers to all the different squiggles and patterns that make up the written alphabet of a language. However, the same script can often be used for multiple languages. Take for example, the Indian script of Devanagari. It is used to write Hindi, Sanskrit, Marathi and many other languages. Or take the Latin script which is used for English, French, German and more. Conversely, one language can be written in different scripts. For example, the Japanese language can be written in Kanji, Hiragana or Katakana scripts.

who had made a lot of donations. Once he figured this first word out, he carefully and painstakingly broke the script, little by little, until he could read all of it.

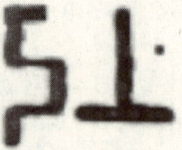

The word *daanam* in the Brahmi script

That is how India got to decipher the Brahmi alphabet – a script that was in use as far back as the third century BCE, nearly 2,300 years ago. Historians say that most scripts used in India today have evolved from this mother script.

But who was this great gift-giving king that Prinsep found out about? The inscriptions referred to this king as 'Devanampiya Piyadasi', a title that means 'Beloved

How did scripts evolve in India? India has 22 official languages and many more are spoken within certain communities. Many of these languages have their own scripts. Those spoken in north India are largely derived from Sanskrit, which is hardly spoken any more, while the languages spoken in south India are all related to Tamil. Today, Tamil is spoken by over 70 million people and is one of the oldest surviving languages in the world.

Did you know that 2,000 years ago, both these ancient languages – Tamil and Sanskrit – used a derivative of the same script? Most epigraphists think that Brahmi is the oldest readable script in India. As early as the third century BCE, Sanskrit was written in the Brahmi script. The old Brahmi script evolved over centuries into the modern Devanagari script, which is used to write Sanskrit, Hindi and many other north Indian languages. The Brahmi script travelled south and was adopted by the Tamil speakers too. But it was adapted to produce certain phonetics not available in Sanskrit. It was called Damili or Tamil Brahmi. That script underwent major changes, particularly in the second and fourth centuries CE. The modern Tamil script evolved around the 16th century. However, not all scholars agree on this north to south theory. Some believe that there was a pre-existing script when Brahmi came south.

But there exists an even older script, referred to as Graffiti, that remains undeciphered to this day. The inscriptions found in the excavations of the Indus Valley civilization, in modern day western and north-western India and Pakistan, were in this script. These inscriptions date back to between 2600 and 1600 BCE.

of the Gods'. Judging by the name, Prinsep assumed that the king was from Sri Lanka. But then, why would a Sri Lankan king carve inscriptions way up in the northern parts of India? That's when Prinsep learned that the Sri Lankan people knew of a great Indian king named Ashoka who also went by the title 'Devanampiya Piyadasi'. More than 2,000 years ago, it was due to Ashoka's efforts that Buddhism had spread to Sri Lanka.

Soon, other experts translated all of Ashoka's writings and discovered many more interesting things about him. Today, our history books are full of the achievements of Ashoka the Great, one of the mightiest kings to have ruled in India. But we may have never known of him, if not for the persistence of the English scholar who was intrigued by the mystery of a lost script.

2

The Temple of Treasures
PADMANABHASWAMY TEMPLE, THIRUVANANTHAPURAM

For centuries, an age-old temple stood
Silently in the midst of lagoons and deep dark woods;
No one knew that underneath the shrine
Lay secret vaults richer than a gold mine!
And when the vaults were opened, the story unfurled
That this was the richest temple in the whole wide world.

Which is the richest religious body in the world?

That is a very difficult question to answer, because much of the wealth of many religious bodies is intangible and almost impossible to value. But going by bankers' estimates, the richest religious body was believed to be the city-state of Vatican, with its priceless historical treasures and invaluable artwork collections.

The richest temple in India, at least until a decade ago, was believed to be the Venkateswara Temple in Tirupati in Andhra Pradesh.

And then, in 2011, an ancient temple in Thiruvananthapuram, the Padmanabhaswamy Temple, burst into the picture. For centuries before this, the temple had existed quietly, tucked away amidst the

As is the case with many religious bodies, the precise net worth of Vatican too is not known; we only have directional estimates made by experts. The wealth of the Vatican referred to in this story pertains only to the assets of the city-state of Vatican, and not of the Roman Catholic Church worldwide. The Roman Catholic Church oversees dioceses across the world, but each individual diocese manages its own wealth. Most of the church's wealth is thus outside the Vatican and in many cases includes sizeable real-estate holdings.

lagoons and coconut trees of Kerala. It came into the limelight because a person working in the temple complained to the Kerala High Court that the temple funds were being mismanaged. The court ordered that, as a first step, all the temple assets be listed out in detail.

Padmanabhaswamy Temple

The idol of the holy deity inside the sanctum sanctorum is unique. It is not made of stone or metal as is common in Dravidian temples. The core is made of wood from the *iluppai* tree, a common tropical tree found in many states of India. It is believed to have medicinal properties. It has been coated with a thick herbal paste known as *katu-sarkara-yogam*. The process of making this paste involves mixing 108 natural materials like jaggery, resin from specific trees, oil, coconut husk and riverine sand, among many other ingredients. They are mixed in specific proportions, and in a specific sequence, as detailed in ancient sculpture manuals called the *Shilpa Sasthra*s. The idol is studded with 12,008 *shaligram* stones. These stones are fossils of ammonite shells formed millions of years ago. These were harvested from the River Gandaki in Nepal and are considered holy. Very few temples contain idols of this composition. Because of this, the idol is never given the daily ritual bath ('*abhishekam*'), unlike in most other temples. The *abhishekam* is performed on a different idol instead.

And so a group of auditors went deep into the underground chambers of the temple where the vaults were located. They had no idea how many surprises were awaiting them! They had been told that there were only six vaults. They found two more. When they entered the secret vaults with torches, they could not believe their eyes. Precious stones and jewellery were lying scattered all over the floor – including a necklace of pure gold that was 18 feet long, a golden throne studded with diamonds, hundreds of gold chains and thousands of golden pots, overflowing with ancient coins! They found Medieval, Roman and pre-Christian era coins, some dating as far back as 200 BCE! A ballpark estimate indicates that there is over 1,300 tonnes of gold in there. Add all of its other treasures and the net worth of this temple is *conservatively* estimated at a whopping USD 40 billion (approximately 300,000 crore rupees). And that is just the material value. Most of these items are antiques and are therefore priceless.

But how did this temple come into so much wealth?

Kerala was always a wealthy state. It had been trading with Arabia, Europe and Africa for at least 2,000 years. Much of the excess wealth found its way into the temple, as offerings to the gods.

Also, for centuries, the rich rulers of south India, including the Cheras, Pandyas, Cholas, Pallavas and the Travancore kings, had been giving gifts to this famous temple. Even after wars, when new kings took over, this royal patronage would continue. After all, these were their gods too.

Later, between the 17th and 19th centuries, Hindu rulers seeking refuge from invading armies were often allowed to settle in Travancore. They too contributed their wealth to the temple.

And then in 1750, something very significant happened. On 18 January 1750, Marthanda Varma, the then king of Travancore, walked into the Padmanabhaswamy Temple and placed his personal sword, the symbol of his power, at the feet of the Lord. He declared that everything he owned, including the kingdom itself, now belonged to the Lord and that he, the king, was only the custodian. With that one act, the deity in the temple, Lord Padmanabhaswamy, officially became the king of Travancore. Marthanda Varma now took on the role of an administrator, managing the kingdom on behalf of Padmanabhaswamy. From then on, all his successors have followed suit and officially remained mere administrators.

This transfer of power from the king to God, called the 'Thrippadi Daanam', is a defining moment in the history of Kerala. Kerala promotes itself as 'God's own country' – and this event makes it almost literally true! From 1750 onwards, God was officially the king

Why did Marthanda Varma give away his kingdom to God? Marthanda Varma had to overcome much internal dissent to establish himself firmly on the throne. The clever decision to offer Thrippadi Daanam sent out many messages. From then on, an enemy of the king was an enemy of God himself. No one dared to challenge him, because that meant challenging God's primary servant. Anything said or done against the king would be seen as an act against God. Meanwhile, his reign continued undisturbed and it was business as usual in the palace.

Marthanda Varma – Thrippadi Daanam

of Kerala. This also meant that all of Kerala's wealth became God's personal wealth, and so it stayed quietly hidden away in the temple vaults. All this wealth has been slowly collecting there for centuries.

Even the British recognized this shift in power. Every time the idol of Padmanabhaswamy was taken out on a procession, it was accorded a 21-gun salute by the

How old is the Padmanabhaswamy Temple?
Nobody knows its exact age. The inscriptions in the sanctum are in Tamil – in an ancient obsolete script called Vattezhuthu. This script originally evolved after the fourth century and was popular in Kerala even in the 12th century. However, we do know that Marthanda Varma (r. 1729–58) completely revamped the temple. Its current architectural style is a fusion of Keralite and Dravidian styles.

British – an honour they normally reserved for a select few Indian kings.

The Thrippadi Daanam created new traditions that are followed to this day. There's a rule that the king must visit the temple every day to give an account of all administrative activities of the kingdom. If he fails to visit the temple, he has to pay a fine – a princely sum of about 150 rupees per day.

Three hundred years after Thrippadi Daanam, Padmanabhaswamy continues to call the shots in Thiruvananthapuram. In 1932, when the new airport was being commissioned, the then ruler of Travancore, Maharaja Sree Chithira Thirunal Balarama Varma, generously donated land for its construction. The piece of land came with one condition. Traditionally, twice a year, the temple idol is taken in a procession to the beach. It so happens that the procession has to cut through the airport to reach the beach, its final destination. In fact, the new runway came up right on the procession path. Did the procession change its route? Of course not! The king insisted that these processions must continue as before, even after the construction of the airport. So twice a year, the Thiruvananthapuram airport is shut down for five full hours, allowing the procession to go through. It is the Kingdom of Gods after all, and they wait for no aeroplanes!

Let's go back to our story of the treasure. What happens to all this wealth now? Does it remain with God? After all, it was given to him. Does it belong to the descendants of the Travancore kings? After all, it was

Procession of the temple idol

their wealth that they passed on to Padmanabhaswamy. Does it go back to the people? After all, they were the ones who gave it to the kings in the first place. Or does it go to the government?

It is no surprise that this weighty matter landed up in the courts. And, recently, the court upheld the rights of the Travancore royal family to continue as administrators of the temple treasure, with many conditions. For now, all that wealth is safe, locked up in the underground vaults. And for all we know, it could stay that way for a very long time.

But there is one more exciting detail in this story. There is still one vault in the temple that remains locked: Vault B. No one knows what is inside. It seems that the doors of this particular vault have an image of a snake carved on it. That is considered a symbol of ill-omen and the priests of the temple insist that terrible things will happen if it is opened. So no one has dared to open it, yet.

What secrets could it be hiding? Evil spirits? Or more unimaginable wealth? We may never know.

3

The Arrival of Christianity in India

SANTHOME BASILICA, CHENNAI

Two thousand years ago, a man came to India from distant lands;
He landed in Kerala, then left his footprints on Chennai's sands.
He brought a new religion, which lodged and took root –
A religion that came in waves, with many an offshoot.
Many flocked to hear him speak, and some went on to
follow his way –
Their descendants are among the oldest Christians in the
world today.

Only 2.5 per cent of India's population is Christian. But then, Christianity did come into India fairly recently, didn't it? Or did it? When exactly did Christianity reach India? And who brought the religion to the country?

It all started about 2,000 years ago in Jerusalem. It is believed that Jesus Christ was crucified there in 33 CE. Soon after, the Apostles – eleven of his closest disciples – cast lots to decide where each of them would travel to speak about Christ. One of the Apostles was St Thomas, and he picked India. His journey was a long one: from the Mediterranean, he travelled via the Red Sea and then to the Arabian Sea. Finally, he landed in Kerala, on

Santhome Basilica

the western coast of India. There, he spoke to people about Christ and his message. His talks were said to be popular, and people flocked to listen to him. Not long afterwards, the first churches in India were established in the region. A 'church' in this context does not mean the grand structure we are used to seeing today. Instead, it refers to a group of people who accepted that Christ was indeed the Messiah.

The descendants of this early group of Christians are called the Thomas Christians or Mar Thoma Christians. They took to Christianity sometime between 52 CE and 72 CE. *That* is how old Christianity is in India.

This makes India one of the first countries where Christianity took root.

Do you know the name of the first European country that adopted Christianity as a state religion? It was Armenia, and it did so in 301 CE – a good 250 years after Christianity came to India. The Thomas Christians of Kerala are considered to be among the oldest practising Christians in the world.

A few years after landing in Kerala, St Thomas is said to have walked across the peninsula and reached the shores of Mylapore, in present-day Chennai. He lived in a place, which is today called Little Mount, and would go down to the beach, a few kilometres away, to meet people and talk about Christ. Here too his speeches were extremely popular – so much so that even the king of the land is said to have come to listen to him.

Unfortunately, all that popularity earned St Thomas some enemies. One day when he was praying at Little Mount, he was attacked and had to flee for his life. The story goes that he met his end on a hillock nearby that is today called St Thomas Mount. This was in 72 CE. His body was then taken down to the beach where he used to preach, and he was buried in Mylapore, in a place now called the Santhome Basilica in Chennai.

For the next 1,400 years, most people forgot about St Thomas. But every once in a while, small groups of Christians from Persia, Armenia and other Middle Eastern lands – largely Nestorian Christians – would come to Chennai and revive memories of the Apostle.

There have been several attempts to take the remains of St Thomas to Europe. The bones were first taken to Edessa in Upper Mesopotamia, now a part of Turkey, then Chios in Greece and finally Ortona in Italy. St Thomas is celebrated in all these places, and his relics are still treasured in Edessa and Chios. But Chennai has the honour of having a basilica built over the tomb. What is a basilica? It is a church that has been specially designated as such by the Pope, because of its religious or historical significance. The tomb chapel at Santhome Basilica has a relic of St Thomas on display – a small fragment of a bone believed to be from the saint's hand.

The Nestorians were followers of Nestorius, a fifth century archbishop of Constantinople who broke away from the church of the Roman Empire, because of ideological differences.

Now, how much of this story is accurate? It is difficult to say. When talking about an incident from such a long time ago, it is often difficult to draw clear lines between history, myths and faith – all of which tend to get beautifully intertwined over time.

But we can be more certain of all that happened since the 1500s, when the Portuguese first came to Chennai, to trade. It is believed that the Armenian Christians, who lived and traded in Chennai, led the Portuguese to the tomb. After all, the eastern Christians had already been visiting the tomb for centuries by then. The Portuguese, who were devout Catholics, were delighted to find the

Have you ever heard the phrase 'Doubting Thomas'? It comes from the biblical story of St Thomas's refusal to believe in the resurrection of Jesus Christ. After the crucifixion, Jesus Christ is said to have risen and appeared before his Apostles. St Thomas was away at that time, and when the others told him about it, he flatly refused to believe them. Eight days later, Jesus appeared again – in the presence of St Thomas this time; to quell his Apostle's disbelief, he even invited St Thomas to see and feel his wounds. The phrase 'Doubting Thomas' has therefore come to refer to people who refuse to believe anything without proof.

The Bleeding Cross

How does one piece together the life of a person who lived nearly 2,000 years ago? Sometimes, accidental discoveries from far-flung places add a lot to our knowledge.

In 1945, in a little village in Egypt called Nag Hammadi, two brothers were ploughing their field when they stumbled upon a sealed earthen jar that contained a few old books. Neither of the brothers thought much of their find and so they didn't bother to report it. Their mother however, discovered a good use for these manuscripts. She found that they made excellent fuel for her oven! As for the brothers, whenever they found an interested buyer, they sold off a few books.

Eventually, one of these books found its way to a museum in Cairo. And that was when they discovered that the books dated to the third and fourth centuries. Today, the museum has 11 of the original books, with fragments of the others. One of the books that managed to survive in its entirety is *The Gospel of Thomas*, which tells stories of the saint and of his interactions with Jesus.

There is another source of information about the life of St Thomas as well – a book called the *Acta Thomae*, also written in the third century CE. It is from this book that we know that St Thomas reached India. It is believed that he reached what is today's Afghanistan and it seems Christianity took root *there* first. He then travelled down to north-west India and took the sea route from there to land in Kerala.

But how genuine are these stories? We don't really know. There are arguments for both sides, and many interpretations of these finds. The Catholic church has declared these books as apocryphal, meaning that it considers them to be of doubtful authenticity.

tomb of an Apostle, no less! And so they built a small Portuguese-style church over the tomb.

Then in the 1600s, the British reached Chennai. They were a powerful force and very soon ended up controlling the entire Bay of Bengal coastline. In the 1890s, they decided to rebuild the Portuguese church in their own style. And that is the beautiful neo-Gothic cathedral that we know today as St Thomas Cathedral Basilica. This church has a special significance. There are only three churches in the world that are built on the remains of an Apostle of Jesus Christ, and St Thomas Basilica is one of them.

> The other two churches built over the remains of an Apostle are St Peter's Basilica in the Vatican and the Santiago de Compostela Cathedral in Spain, where the relics of St James are buried.

4

The Richest Company of All Time

VOC GATE, FORT KOCHI

A private company with forty warships
And an army of ten thousand men –
A company that was mightier than
Many European kingdoms back then;
So powerful that it defeated a country
And took over its lands…
And it all began with a set of stolen maps
That fell into the wrong hands!

In 1663, Kochi became the capital of Dutch India. For the next 100 years, the Dutch controlled large tracts of spice-rich Kerala from there. But behind that Dutch success lies the story of a remarkable private company that went on to become the richest company there ever was. That company was the VOC.

If you visit Kochi, you can see the logo of this company on the VOC Gate in the Parade Ground of Fort Kochi. VOC stood for 'Vereenigde Oostindische Compagnie', commonly known as the Dutch East India Company. It was established in 1602, and it was the first ever company listed on a stock exchange.

The British East India Company was set up even earlier than the VOC – in 1600, as a privately held company under a royal charter. But its shares began to be traded in public much later.

In the mid–15th century, Portugal and Spain were the superpowers of Europe. Both had powerful navies and were eager to conquer new territories and expand their markets. Naturally, they quarrelled. The one person who could mediate was the Pope, the religious leader of Catholics all over the world. Portugal and Spain were both devoutly Catholic nations, and therefore held the Pope in the highest regard. Alexander VI, who was the Pope at that time, stepped in to settle the dispute. He divided the world into two, and gave the Portuguese exclusive rights to all the lands in the East – essentially, Africa and Asia. And he gave the Spanish exclusive rights to all the lands in the West – meaning North and South America.

The interesting thing here was that the Pope was partitioning lands over which he had no authority at all! Moreover, at the time, no one in Europe, including the Pope himself, knew where or just how big these lands were.

Portugal immediately set its sights on India. After all, India was the hub of the spice trade and trading in spices was very lucrative. It is estimated that in 1500 CE, in Portugal, a kilogram of pepper was worth two kilograms

VOC Gate

of gold! And so the Portuguese sent an expedition under the command of their explorer Vasco da Gama and established a new sea route to India. This was followed by more expeditions, and soon Portugal had set up a string of colonies all along the Indian coastline. Many coastal kingdoms in India had no choice but to submit to the Portuguese navy, because the latter had superior gun power. Goa became the capital of Portuguese India.

Portugal acquired a monopoly over the Indian spice trade and made enormous profits from its Indian colonies. For about a hundred years, no one challenged the monopoly. Why? Because no one knew the sea route to India except Portugal, which was certainly not going to share its maps with anyone. The maps were a closely guarded secret.

Things changed dramatically in the 1600s, though, when two new superpowers emerged in Europe: Holland and England. These were Protestant nations that did not view the Pope as a religious head. So they paid no heed to his orders. They too had strong navies with the capability of sailing to India. All they needed were the maps. If only they could get a sneak peek into those Portuguese maps! The opportunity to gain access came in an unexpected way. And what they got was not merely a peek, but an eyeful!

In the 1580s, the head of the Portuguese Church in Goa, Archbishop Fonseca, was a very powerful man. He had a Dutch secretary named Jan Huyghen van Linschoten. Archbishop Fonseca blindly trusted

Jan Huyghen and gave him full access to all official Portuguese records in Goa. These archives included all maps of sea routes from Europe to India, China and Japan. Jan Huyghen was smart enough to realize the value of these documents. So when he got the chance, he meticulously copied down every one of them. The Portuguese officials were blissfully unaware of what was happening under their noses.

When the Archbishop died in 1587, Jan Huyghen quietly left Goa with copies of these secret documents. He reached Holland, and between 1595 and 1596, he went on to publish books that contained all the secret maps he had stolen. The secret that the Portuguese had so jealously guarded for nearly a century was now freely available on the streets of Europe!

The Dutch trading community immediately grabbed the opportunity. Soon, many adventurous merchants from Holland were sending ships to India. Some made huge profits, but it was a risky journey. One sunk ship could ruin a merchant for life. But then the Dutch came up with a brilliant idea to protect their interests.

In 1602, all the Dutch merchants pooled their resources together and formed the world's first multinational company called the United Dutch East India Company, or the VOC. The Dutch government gave it monopoly rights to operate in the East. This meant that the company could colonize territories, negotiate treaties with local kings, wage wars, convict and execute prisoners, and even mint its own coins.

One of the first actions of the VOC navy was to practise organized piracy against the Portuguese. In February 1603, a fleet of VOC ships patrolling the sea near Singapore attacked the *Santa Catarina*, a Portuguese merchant vessel. The Portuguese crew was disarmed and the ship looted. They got a rich haul of Chinese silk, Ming porcelain, musk and other valuables. They hauled in so much loot that the lighter Dutch ships had to dump some of their cargo. But the silk alone was worth 2.2 million guilders (the old Dutch currency) and the total loot covered nearly 50 per cent of VOC's paid-up capital. For many years after, it was standard practice to loot Portuguese ships. In the early years this alone brought in enormous profits to VOC.

This was clearly not a 'legitimate' activity, but most VOC shareholders accepted the loot with glee. A handful of the more orthodox shareholders objected. But piracy was bringing in so much money that the majority shareholders silenced them.

Portugal of course cried that it was a hostile act. But it did not matter: Holland and Portugal were already at war. Moreover, the Portuguese indignation was hardly righteous: the Dutch did to the Portuguese what the Portuguese had been doing all along to other nations!

It was a state within a state. To enforce its enormous authority, it had 40 warships and a standing army of at least 10,000 men. A private company was basically now fully equipped to fight naval battles with Portugal!

Soon, Dutch ships were all over the Indian coast, mercilessly harassing Portuguese shipping. The Portuguese ships also had to fend of English attacks. But Portugal had even bigger problems to deal with. By then, Portugal had become a vassal state of Spain and its maritime power was declining. Not long afterwards, the Portuguese had to give up almost every Indian colony they owned.

And what did fate have in store for the Dutch and the VOC? The VOC made such enormous profits that it went on to become the largest ever multinational company in history. At its peak, it was worth USD 7.9 trillion at current prices. How big is that? Put together

The Bolgatty Palace in Kochi is a beautiful example of Dutch colonial architecture and is one of the oldest Dutch palaces outside Holland. The Dutch governor of colonial India stayed here, and later it was home to British governors. Between 1604 and 1639, the Dutch continuously harassed the Portuguese near Goa, but could not capture it. So they focused on the Portuguese settlements in Kerala. Slowly, the VOC forces wrested many Portuguese strongholds like Quilon and Cranganore. But Kochi, a strategic kingdom, was under a king who was friendly with the Portuguese. The Dutch VOC army deposed and killed him, using the support of a rebel royal faction. Then they installed a Dutch-friendly royal as king, and Kochi became the capital of Dutch India from 1663. The Bolgatty Palace is now a luxury hotel.

the top 20 companies of today, including Apple, Amazon, Microsoft and the Bank of America among others, and it would still be *smaller* than the VOC of the time. In fact, the VOC was bigger and more powerful than many small European kingdoms!

In 1741, the Dutch were defeated by a king from Kerala. By this time, Britain had become the bigger power in India. So the Dutch decided to shift their spice trade from India to Indonesia. About 40 years after this, the VOC was taken over by the Dutch government and all the territories it had acquired became Dutch colonies. Then on 31 December 1799, the VOC itself was dissolved, marking the end of the largest and most successful multinational company ever. And to think that it all began with a bunch of stolen maps!

5

Stone Caskets with the Buddha's Remains

THE GREAT STUPA, SANCHI

Eight ancient kingdoms fought over the Buddha's remains —
His ashes, hair, teeth, bones and nails;
They divided the relics, buried them deep underground
And magnificent stupas got built over the mounds.
There they remained inside caskets of stone
Until a mighty king placed them in caskets of his own;
These chipped stone caskets with the relics inside
Helped revive Buddhism, and spread it far and wide.

Stone caskets

Did you know that some Buddhist temples in South and South-East Asia have stone caskets that contain the cremated remains of Lord Buddha himself? This is a story about them. It takes us to the Sanchi Stupa in Madhya Pradesh, and it is about the events that followed the death of Gautama Buddha, nearly 2,500 years ago.

Buddhism is sometimes called an atheistic religion. During his lifetime, the Buddha never called himself God and he did not speak about praying to gods either. He just taught people the importance of living a righteous life.

So his earliest followers looked upon him as an enlightened teacher and never worshipped his image. In fact, for centuries after the Buddha's death, it was forbidden to create his idols or images. Instead, sculptors of the time used various symbols to represent the Buddha and inspire devotees – the Buddha's footprints, his begging bowl, and more common symbols like the lotus and the wheel. The lotus and the wheel are sacred symbols in Hinduism and Jainism too.

Why are the lotus and the wheel considered sacred in Buddhism? The symbolic message is that just as a lotus rises out of slushy waters, one must rise above earthly desires to realize the purity of the soul. The wheel usually has eight spokes, symbolizing the eight-fold path that the Buddha advocated: Right View, Right Intention, Right Speech, Right Action, Right Livelihood, Right Effort, Right Mindfulness and Right Samadhi (meditation).

The Buddha is believed to have died in 483 BCE in Kushinagara, in the kingdom of the Mallas in north India. His body was cremated immediately after his death. But his ashes and other relics – his hair, teeth, nails and bones – were safely preserved for future generations to draw inspiration from them.

At that time, there were seven other kingdoms that venerated the Buddha equally – Rajagriha, Vaishali, Kapilavastu, Allakappa, Ramagrama, Vethadvipa and Pava. They too wanted a share of his relics, and so a war broke out between the eight kingdoms. Finally, as a compromise, the ashes were divided into eight stone caskets and distributed amongst the warring kings. Each of the kings buried the casket in their capital city and built a stupa over it. In Sanskrit, 'stupa' means a heap or mound.

Some 2,000 years later, in 1818, a British major general, James Taylor of the Bengal Cavalry, was patrolling some hilly jungles near Bhopal, now in Madhya Pradesh. He was on the lookout for a group of bandits who were terrorizing that region. That's when he unexpectedly stumbled upon the ruins of a 2,000-year-old monument that had been 'lost' for over 500 years – the Sanchi Stupa. He reported his discovery and moved on; it would be another 100 years before the world understood the magnitude of Taylor's discovery. Today, we know that it is one of the oldest stone monuments in India and a very important Buddhist shrine. More importantly, it is from the stone

Sanchi Stupa

panels on the southern gateway of the Sanchi Stupa that historians were able to piece together the events that followed the Buddha's death.

Not long after, in the 1830s, another Englishman, a man named James Prinsep (yes, the same one we met in the first chapter) managed to decipher an ancient Indian script called Brahmi. This long-forgotten script, you will remember, was found on 2,000-year-old stone pillars across India. Historians could now read those inscriptions. And that is how India was introduced to its greatest Buddhist king, Emperor Ashoka.

Ashoka was crowned the king of the Mauryan Empire in 268 BCE, about 200 years after the death of the Buddha. He ruled over large parts of the subcontinent. At one point in his life, he became a Buddhist and started spreading the religion with great zeal. That's when he found that many old Buddhist shrines and stupas were falling to ruin. If Buddhism had to be rejuvenated, it needed monuments that would remind the common folk of the Buddha and his teachings. Ashoka remembered those eight caskets containing the Buddha's relics. In an inspired moment, he retrieved the caskets, and divided their contents into 84,000 smaller caskets. He had them buried in stupas all over India and other Asian countries.

The Sanchi Stupa is one of the oldest stone structures in India. But what you see there today was NOT built by Ashoka. The original stupa built by the king was made of bricks. A few years after Ashoka's death, Pushyamitra Shunga, a Hindu general, overthrew the Maurya dynasty and declared himself king. Historians think that he vandalized the original Sanchi Stupa. They also believe that Pushyamitra's son, Agnimitra, rebuilt a larger stone stupa over the old one. The beautiful ornamental gates around the stupa, called *toranas*, were built by later Hindu kings called the Satavahanas. And some of the shrines on the campus were built by Hindu Gupta kings who ruled in a later period. Isn't it amazing that this much venerated Buddhist monument was almost entirely sponsored by Hindus? There is hardly anything of Ashoka's at Sanchi, except for the brilliant original inspiration.

One of those 84,000 caskets was placed in a stupa at Sanchi – the same one that the English general discovered by accident. This stupa had a special significance in Ashoka's life. Before becoming king, Ashoka had been the viceroy of the Ujjain province, of which Sanchi was a part. Sanchi was where Ashoka met and married his wife, Devi. Devi was a Buddhist, and many historians think she may have been a factor in his conversion to Buddhism. It is said that the construction of the Sanchi Stupa was supervised by Queen Devi herself. Gradually, Sanchi became an important Buddhist centre. Pilgrims from many faraway lands began travelling to Sanchi.

After Ashoka's death in 232 BCE, the Sanchi Stupa was destroyed and reconstructed by subsequent dynasties. Two Hindu dynasties, the Satavahanas and the Guptas, added beautiful Buddhist monuments to the site. The stone stupa we see today was built over the older one, which was made of brick. Over the next 1,000 years, the religious landscape in India changed. Buddhism slowly declined and the stupas fell into ruin. Sanchi remained a place of active worship until the ninth century, when the last temple was constructed on the campus. By the 13th century, the complex itself was forgotten, completely hidden by the trees and shrubs that grew thickly around it.

So where can we find the Buddha's caskets and original relics today? Remember the 84,000 caskets of relics that

Ashoka did not get his hands on all eight original caskets. He had to leave one out. The Ramagrama Stupa in Nepal was guarded by a fierce race of Nagas who flatly refused to part with their casket. There was nothing Ashoka could do to persuade them; so till date, that continues to be the only stupa with the original casket still intact.

Ashoka distributed? Some of them may be lost forever, while some might have been further redistributed. Today, many South and South-East Asian countries claim to have the Buddha's relics. These are all important pilgrimage sites for Buddhists now, and Buddhism continues to thrive in many of these countries. Sanchi is now a UNESCO World Heritage site and a pilgrimage centre for Buddhists across the world.

But none of it would have happened, if not for the foresight of one Indian king and the resilience of these chipped stone caskets that have represented the Buddha for nearly 2,500 years!

6

The Coolest Building
in the Country

MADRAS ICE HOUSE, CHENNAI

On Marina Beach in Madras stands
A charming circular building that demands
A second look, for it is oddly shaped and old,
Reminding us of an enterprise outrageously bold.

Ice House

The British East India Company arrived in Madras, today's Chennai, in 1639. They raised a fort here and established a permanent settlement for themselves.

But life wasn't easy for an Englishman living in Madras then. Language was a huge barrier, mosquitoes were plentiful and there was of course the unrelenting heat. The British never learnt to deal with it; even in the searing summers of Madras, they dressed in the typical English fashion of the time – tight pantaloons, a shirt with a high collar, waistcoat, overcoat and, if one were important enough, even a wig, top hat and gloves!

At the end of the day, they must have yearned for something cold. Perhaps a tall glass of fresh juice, clinking with ice? But alas, refrigeration had not been invented yet.

In the early 1800s, there lived an enterprising young American named Frederic Tudor. He was from Boston (in the US), a region that has many freshwater lakes. And in winter these lakes freeze over and become vast expanses of ice! Tudor saw all that ice one day and had a eureka moment. He figured that there was much money to be made by harvesting that ice and selling it in places with warmer climates. He found a way to cut and scoop up the ice from the lakes, loaded it on a cargo ship and took it to Havana, in tropical Cuba. It was a maverick idea that was modestly successful. But it made him dream bigger. He decided to ship ice to India. After all, India was hotter, bigger and richer! But would the ice survive the four-month voyage largely over warm tropical seas?

When he first started shipping ice, Tudor had grossly underestimated the marketing challenge that lay before him. People who needed ice did *not know* that they needed it. In the early stages of his business, he sent a shipment of ice to the island of Martinique in the West Indies. The ice reached safely, but the locals were hardly interested. They had no idea that they could chill their drinks with ice, nor did they have a taste for it.

So Tudor went from bar to bar, offering free ice to customers. Slowly people started appreciating and getting addicted to the idea of chilled drinks. At restaurants, he promoted ice-cream recipes. He caught the imagination of the rich by recommending ice in their bathtubs in summer. By the time Tudor died, it is said that two of three houses in New York had access to retail ice delivery.

Tudor had another idea. New England had many lumber factories. A waste product of these factories was pinewood sawdust, and the owners were glad to give it away at no cost. Tudor collected this sawdust and covered his ice blocks carefully with thick layers of it. This worked as a very effective insulator. In May 1833, a ship left Boston with 180 tonnes of ice. Four months and 26,000 kilometres later, almost 100 tonnes reached Calcutta (now Kolkata) – enough to make a good profit. Calcutta welcomed the cold cargo with great warmth.

The British were thrilled by the windfall; they just couldn't have enough of this ice! They even declared a local holiday to celebrate the arrival of ice. The ice from Boston caused such a sensation that within three days, the local community raised funds to build an ice house in Calcutta! The building was a double-walled, windowless structure, specially designed to store ice.

When Tudor first started harvesting ice around 1805, his idea wasn't exactly a runaway success. His earliest ice shipping trips failed because there was no place to store the ice when his ships docked. So all the ice *and* his profits simply melted away. In fact, he even spent time in prison twice because he couldn't repay his debts.

But Tudor persisted because, intuitively, it made economic sense. The ice was free, and so was the sawdust. Even shipping was cheap, because after ships unloaded their cargo at the Boston port, many would go back empty. They were willing to transport any cargo, including ice, at far cheaper rates. The only challenge was to prevent the ice from melting on the way. Once Tudor perfected the sawdust insulation technique, he had a profit-making proposition.

Soon, ice houses were constructed in Bombay and Madras too.

By the mid-1830s, Tudor was shipping huge quantities of ice to Calcutta, Bombay (now Mumbai) and Madras. India became Tudor's most lucrative destination, and made him very, very rich. For the next 20 years, Tudor reigned as the 'Ice King' of Boston.

By 1860, ice-making machines had been invented. Why import ice from America when you could make it in your own backyard? Tudor's profits evaporated and his business shut down! But Tudor had already made his money by then; he died a rich man in 1864.

Tudor sold his ice to hospitals, where it soon became a necessity for many doctors. One such medical practitioner was Dr John Gorrie who used Tudor's ice for his malaria patients. He experimented further and went on to build his own artificial ice-making machine. Now anyone could make their own ice. Tudor was furious. He mounted a vicious marketing campaign against artificial ice makers and convinced his clients that artificial ice was unhealthy. Dr Gorrie died bankrupt. But better artificial ice-makers soon entered the market and killed the natural ice business. But by then Tudor was already a multimillionaire!

The Ice Houses of Calcutta and Bombay crumbled, but the Ice House of Madras continued to stand resolutely on the Marina.

Today, the Madras Ice House has two floors of arched windows. So how did a once windowless building acquire so many windows?

An Indian lawyer named Biligiri Iyengar bought the Madras Ice House and converted it to a beautiful seaside villa by adding many windows and verandahs. He was a great admirer of Swami Vivekananda – the famous Indian philosopher and nationalist who introduced Western audiences to Indian philosophy, yoga and meditation. In 1897, when Swami Vivekananda returned from a highly successful tour of the US, Iyengar invited Vivekananda to stay in his villa. Vivekananda obliged and stayed over for some days. Soon a branch of the Ramakrishna Mission, a spiritual order established by Swami Vivekananda, began operations from this villa.

Today, the building is a museum, showcasing the life and teachings of Swami Vivekananda. And what used to be the Madras Ice House is now called Vivekanandar Illam or the Vivekananda House.

The Madras Ice House was built in 1842 as a double-walled, windowless, circular warehouse. It was built by a military engineer and was designed to provide insulation to keep the ice from melting. Ice gives out moisture and that would rot wood. So no wood was used in its construction, not even for the roof beams. When Biligiri Iyengar acquired it around 1880, he added the circular verandahs and windows to make it inhabitable. He named it Castle Kernan – after a High Court Judge whom he admired. After his death it was used as a widows' hostel, and later a teachers' hostel for many years. Finally, it was acquired by the government.

7

Village Gods of Tamil Nadu

MARIAMMAN TEMPLE, SAMAYAPURAM

Fearsome looks, armed to the teeth —
You may not have imagined gods this way,
But these are gods from a simpler time,
When even gods had precise roles to play;
They guard the village and heal the sick —
Their role dictates their form.
A walk on hot coals is part of the worship
And ritual sacrifice is quite often the norm.

Tamil Nadu is famous for its temples. The second richest temple in Tamil Nadu (after the Palani Murugan Temple) is the Mariamman Temple in Samayapuram. That's a name many in north India may be unfamiliar with. But down south, in Tamil Nadu, Mariamman is one of the most popular goddesses. Who exactly is Mariamman, and why is she not commonly seen in temples in other parts of India? Perhaps it's because Mariamman is a village goddess.

Do you know how many gods there are in Hinduism? Some put the number at a very specific 330 million, while other scholars insist that there is just one — who is

Where did this number 330 million come from?
Ask a scholar and he might tell you that the right number
is 33, and not 330 million. The Rig Veda speaks of
33 'kotis' of Hindu gods. Somewhere down the line,
perhaps things got lost in translation. 'Koti' in Sanskrit
means 10 million. So 33 kotis adds up to 330 million
gods. But 'koti' also means classes or groups. And
many historians think that is what it referred to.

formless and shapeless. You are free to give this God any
form or shape you like – a tree, an idol, a star or even
a stone. In different parts of India, the same gods go by
different names, each time with a different personality
and a different backstory. So 330 million is not such an
improbable number.

Aiyanar (*back*) and Karuppuswamy

Of all these gods, many today consider three to be the most powerful: Brahma is the god of creation, Shiva the god of destruction, and Vishnu is the god of protection. But then, we are talking of only the Vedic gods. There is another set of deities that is not included in the 330 million: the village gods.

Think of an image of any Hindu god. Curling moustaches; dark, stocky bodies; and armed to the teeth – does this fit your idea of a god? That may not be what you imagined, but take a drive through rural Tamil Nadu and, at the entrance to many villages, you will spot colourful mud horses with fearsome men riding atop them. These are village gods. Locally they are known as 'Kaval Deivam', or guardian spirits. They are worshipped as protectors of the village.

Unlike the Vedic gods who are worshipped across India, village gods are unique to just a small place. While the Vedic gods carry the burden of protecting the whole world, and have huge volumes of sacred literature dedicated to them, village gods are remembered only in local folklore and village songs. But these gods are believed to have existed since pre-Vedic times – for over 3,500 years!

A long time ago, when a man died in battle, villagers would often put up a memorial stone in his honour. Historians believe that over time, some of these hero-stones turned into shrines and the heroes themselves turned into deities. Villagers place a lot of faith in these deities and trust them to take care of their everyday

There are many famous temples dedicated to Tamil Nadu's village gods scattered across South-East Asia, especially in Malaysia and Singapore. As early as the seventh century CE, a Hindu empire called the Srivijaya Empire ruled over parts of South-East Asia. During the rule of the Pallava and Chola kings, more and more Tamil traders came and settled in the Malay Peninsula. By the 19th century, the British East India Company had found a toehold in Singapore. They needed labourers to help them with trade and agricultural activities. Initially, Indian prisoners were brought to Singapore, followed by coolies and labourers from south India – specifically from Tamil Nadu. Along with them, came a clutch of moneylenders, traders and bankers. They all took their language and customs with them. They built small shrines for the gods they brought from their respective villages. This gave the migrants a feeling of security in a strange new land. Even today, these temples continue to be the centre of religious, social and cultural life for the large population of Tamils settled in those lands. There are Mariamman temples in Mauritius, Vietnam, Thailand, Singapore, Malaysia, Fiji, Indonesia, Sri Lanka, Pakistan and many countries in the Caribbean. For the people of her village, Mariamman has travelled the globe to offer protection!

concerns: too little rain or too much of it; epidemics and crop failure; bandits, burglars and bloodthirsty invaders.

Most of these gods have a distinct role to play and a personality to match. Many of them appear angry and

Hero stone

fearsome. Villagers depend on these divine protectors to fight their battles with evil spirits and to ward off other threats. They created images that looked right for the role. There is no attempt made to polish up their scary images.

Take Karuppusamy for instance. You will always find him grim-faced, wearing a permanent scowl. After all, as a protector, he needs to look his part – more brutal than benevolent. The name 'Karuppusamy' literally means 'Black God'. Offerings to him are usually dark in colour and include iron chains, clubs and swords. Villagers like to make sure that he is always well-armed. Karuppuswamy, in turn, reports to a god named Aiyanar. Aiyanar is the most widely worshipped village god in south India. When the village is fast asleep, it is believed that these two gods go around, keeping a sharp eye out for thieves and evil spirits. Just to help them travel easily, villagers gift these gods with colourfully painted clay horses, elephants and tigers. You will see such terracotta horses in most villages of Tamil Nadu.

Once every year, the entire village comes together to make these clay horses. It begins with a sacrifice of a chicken or a goat, to sanctify the mud used for making the horse. Once the horse is made, it is placed with much fanfare at the village entrance. It's job now is to stand there and help Aiyanar protect the village.

So who is the most powerful of these gods? Well, it is actually a goddess. Mariamman is an ancient goddess in Tamil Nadu. She has the all-important role of protecting the village against smallpox, a deadly disease until a few decades ago. But the Tamil people are not the only ones who worship a supreme goddess

Mariamman

who protects their everyday interests. Sheetala worship
in north India and Maisamma worship in Karnataka,
Maharashtra and Telangana address very similar concerns.

Ritual worship in these village temples is different
from that in Vedic temples. Folk dancing is a big part
of the worship. Extreme acts of penance are a common
sight. Many devotees pierce their tongues and cheeks
with a spear or a trident. Others casually walk on a bed
of hot coals without missing a beat.

Mariamman is also the goddess of rain. In fact, the
old Tamil word for rain is 'Mari'. In the Tamil month of
Aadi, which falls in July, farmers pray to her for heavy
rains. Mariamman is ritually worshipped as Goddess
Earth – fertile and rich with the promise of a good
harvest. A common custom in south India is to gift
glass bangles to pregnant women as a blessing for safe
childbirth. So, in the month of Aadi, villagers gather to
celebrate Mariamman's pregnancy, and lovingly gift her

The Samayapuram Mariamman Temple is believed
to have been built in the 17th century. Mariamman is
considered to be another form of the traditional Hindu
goddess Kali. Like many village deities, the idol in the
sanctum of this temple too is made of earth. And so the
daily ritual bath is performed on another idol made of
stone. Today, this goddess has transcended her rural
identity and attracts devotees from all over.

with the symbolic glass bangles – as they fervently hope and pray for a bountiful harvest.

She also goes by other names like Pechiamman and Kaliamman. Depending on the role she takes, she can be charming and beautiful, or fiery and bloodthirsty.

So are these gods also considered Hindu gods? Well, there are many stories that tie them to the Vedic Gods. A popular story relates to the birth of Aiyanar. They say he was born to Shiva and Vishnu, when Vishnu took the form of a beautiful woman named Mohini. Shiva fell in love with Mohini, and their son was Aiyanar.

Yet, village temples are different. The prayers are usually not in Sanskrit, but in the local language. Sacrifice is the norm, and an offering of a goat or a chicken is fairly common. The rituals of worship are specific to the village and may be performed only by a man from that village. Unlike in the Vedic temples, he is usually not a member of the priestly class; often, he is a potter or a carpenter, who played a role in the creation of the terracotta horses.

But then, these gods come from a time when religion was much simpler – a time when even the gods had very precise roles to play.

8

The King Who Brought the Ganga Down South

GANGAIKONDA CHOLAPURAM

His father was named the king of kings,
Who built a BIG temple that towers over all;
The son proved worthy and did many great things,
Though the temple he built is not quite as tall.
His army and navy travelled far and wide –
To the Maldives, Sri Lanka and the south-eastern side;
The new city he built bears a name that came
From his remarkable campaigns in the Gangetic plains.

A thousand years ago, there lived a powerful king in south India. After he had conquered much of the southern peninsula, he decided to build a grand, new capital city for his empire. He wanted to anoint his city with water from the Ganga – a river that is sacred to all Hindus. A river that was 2,000 kilometres away! But he was determined, so he sent a huge army from Thanjavur in Tamil Nadu on a long expedition to bring back water from the Ganga.

On its way, the army would have to cross many kingdoms, spread across today's Odisha, Madhya Pradesh and Bihar. Would these kingdoms allow an alien army to walk through their lands? Of course not. So our king's army simply conquered every kingdom en route – all the way to modern-day West Bengal and even further into Bangladesh. There, they successfully overthrew the Chandra dynasty and returned, triumphantly carrying the holy water. It was one of the most successful military expeditions in Indian history! All the defeated kings along the route became tribute-paying vassals and trade partners of the conquerors, and the resultant wealth made his empire an economic superpower.

Our story is about Rajendra Chola who ruled the Chola kingdom between 1012 and 1044 CE. He initially ruled from Thanjavur (in present-day Tamil Nadu) and later from his new capital city, named Gangaikonda Cholapuram, which literally means, 'the town of the Chola who took over the Gangetic plains'.

But let's backtrack a bit here. Who exactly were these powerful Cholas?

They were a south Indian dynasty that ruled over a large territory for nearly 1,500 years, beginning from the second century BCE. At their peak in the 11th century, they directly ruled over south India, Maldives and Sri Lanka. They also collected tributes from vassal states in parts of eastern India, Burma, Malaysia, Singapore, Indonesia and Cambodia – that's nearly a million square kilometres! Isn't that incredible? Astonishingly, all this happened in the span of just two generations – Rajaraja Chola and his son Rajendra Chola.

In 985 CE, when Rajaraja became king, the Chola kingdom was much smaller and the Tamil country was split between three warring kingdoms – the Cheras of present-day Kerala, the Pandyas who ruled from Madurai and the Cholas who ruled from Thanjavur. Rajaraja swiftly united all three kingdoms under the Chola banner and even annexed the northern half of Sri Lanka. In 1010 CE, he built the gigantic Brihadeeswara temple, one of the tallest man-made structures of the time. You might know it by its more popular name: the Big Temple. Befittingly, 'Rajaraja' literally means 'the king of kings'.

His son, Rajendra was perhaps even greater, and he built on the foundation laid by his father. In fact, many of Rajaraja's conquests were actually won by Rajendra, who was then serving as the commander of his father's army.

As soon as he became king, Rajendra mopped up all the unfinished business left over from his father's time. He successfully captured the remaining parts of Sri Lanka, and made the island a Chola colony. He crushed the revolts of the Cheras and the Pandyas, and appointed his son as the viceroy of those provinces. He defeated the western Chalukyas who ruled the region that is now modern-day Karnataka. And he brought the present-day Andhra region too under his control by installing his own nephew as the king of Vengi.

Next, Rajendra embarked on his most ambitious expedition: an overseas naval campaign! At that time, much of modern-day Malaysia and Indonesia were ruled by the Srivijaya kings. The Cholas had flourishing trade relations with them. Their ships passed through the Malacca Strait, which the Srivijaya kings controlled, onwards to China and back. During Rajendra's rule, the relationship between these kingdoms soured. One theory suggests that the Srivijayans wanted to compete with the Cholas in the lucrative sea trade with China. They quietly increased the customs duties on Chola ships, deeply affecting the Chola trade.

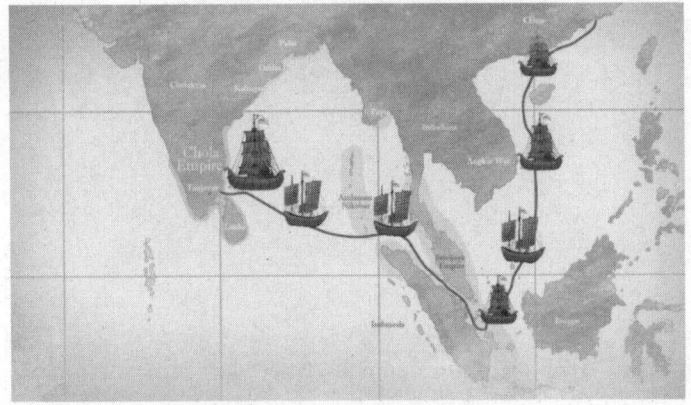

The Chola maritime trade route

Rajendra Chola decided to set things right. He certainly had the right resources. You see, the Cholas were the only dynasty to conceive of a blue-water navy in the history of India. The country has a huge coastline and maritime trade flourished for ages in these parts. But until the Cholas, even the most powerful Indian rulers – the Mauryas, Mughals and Marathas, had only small coastal navies. The Cholas were in a completely different league. Rajendra Chola's navy was estimated to have nearly one million sailors, with hundreds of vessels, spread over several naval bases in coastal Tamil Nadu and northern Sri Lanka. Their predecessors, the Pallavas also had a long-range navy, but the Cholas deployed it to perfection.

Chola ships

In 1025, a huge naval fleet left for Srivijaya. Launching surprise attacks, the Cholas sacked and looted many Srivijayan ports. The Srivijayan king was captured, and the Cholas returned with enormous riches. They did not occupy the defeated territories, but extracted hefty tributes.

This expedition allowed Tamil traders to establish themselves firmly across South-East Asia.

With all that military success behind him, Rajendra decided to build himself a brand-new capital city. Rajendra's army was growing, and each time his army

Rajendra Chola's Srivijaya expedition was remarkable. But what made him invade a kingdom 3,500 kilometres away? Historians offer many different explanations. The Srivijayan coastguard was becoming less effective in checking piracy, and they even probably connived with some pirates. Meanwhile, they increased customs duties, adding to the woes of Chola traders. Chola trade with Cambodia, Thailand and China was getting impacted. It appears that Rajendra's intention was not to annex Srivijaya, but to make their trade policy more favourable to Tamil traders. This was similar to the policy of 'gunboat diplomacy' where European countries used naval power in the 17th and 18th centuries to intimidate Asian kingdoms. There is also another theory that the Khmer King Suryavarman requested Rajendra's help in his fight against a Malay king.

needed to move northwards it had to ford the River Kaveri at least twice. He needed a modern cantonment at a more strategic location. He chose a site on the banks of the River Kollidam and a new city, Gangaikonda Cholapuram, was born.

Works of ancient Tamil literature describe the city in glowing terms. The bustling streets were full of works of art and treasures from foreign lands. The Gangaikonda Cholapuram Temple, the architectural marvel that Rajendra built, could be seen from anywhere in the city. Nearby, Rajendra had a beautiful palace. It remained the Chola capital for the next 250 years, until the fall of the Chola Empire in 1279.

The Gangaikonda Cholapuram Temple is a UNESCO World Heritage monument. It is grouped with the Big Temple of Thanjavur and the Darasuram Temple as one of the 'Great living Chola temples'. For nearly 1,000 years it has withstood the ravages of nature, as well as the depredations of invaders. Its worst crisis was perhaps during the British period when they broke the outer walls, which they then used to build a dam on the River Kollidam. They soon realized their folly and now it is protected by the Archaeological Survey of India (ASI), which has done much conservation work. Although the vimana (tower over the sanctum) is smaller than the Thanjavur Temple, it has a very unique curvilinear shape. The temple walls and towers are packed with exquisite carvings depicting scenes from Indian mythology.

Today, that grand city is but a small town, and the Chola palace is just a mound of bricks. But the Gangaikonda Cholapuram Temple still stands tall, as a charming celebration of the greatest Chola king Rajendra Chola!

There is one other monument that still remains. Rajendra wanted to inspire awe in his people with his conquests. The motivation was not just religious. Bringing Ganga water to his new city added a sense of drama to his achievements, perhaps even suggesting that he had the divine Ganga's blessings. So he built a huge reservoir in his new capital city, poured the holy water into it and called it Chola-Gangam! Today that lake is

Gangaikonda Cholapuram Temple

called Ponneri, and it is still one of the largest man-made lakes in India – even a thousand years after it was built!

Back in those days, a victorious king would commemorate his wins on the battlefield by raising a victory tower called a Jayasthambham. Inscriptions of the time refer to this lake as a Jalasthambham – meaning a water monument meant to celebrate Rajendra Chola's victories over kings in the Gangetic plains. Quite apt, don't you think, for a southern king who brought the mighty Ganga's waters to his backyard?

9

How a Maharaja Crossed the Ocean

CITY PALACE, JAIPUR

An Indian maharaja all set to sail
Was held back by a taboo that prevailed
Until silver vats gave him wings –
An idea that moved coolies and kings.
Soldiers and slaves were shipped far and wide
With the holy Ganga by their side.
This is the story of a taboo and a jail,
And of a clever workaround that let Indians sail.

On the next page is an image of one of the world's largest silver artefacts – the famous Jaipur vats. Following it is the Cellular Jail in Andaman. Can you spot a connection?

Today these huge jars can be found, gleaming quietly, in the City Palace in Jaipur. But in 1901, they travelled halfway across the globe, and hobnobbed with the rich and powerful of the time. They have quite a story to tell.

In the early 1900s, very few Indians travelled overseas. It was expensive, and it came with a very big social risk. Back then, there was a taboo that if Hindus sailed on the seas, they would lose their caste. In many parts of India, people who travelled the oceans were disowned by their

The famous Jaipur silver vat

Cellular Jail

community. Many a time, if at all someone sailed, their last rites would be performed even before they boarded the ship. And when they came back, they could own no property and would have lost their place in their community. This taboo was called *kala pani* (which literally translates as 'black water'). It is difficult to say exactly when and how this taboo originated. But it was

It is not clear when *kala pani* originated. But by the 19th century, the taboo was deeply set. However, there were times when Indians, at least from some parts of the country, were quite comfortable zipping across the oceans for trade. Between the sixth and 11th centuries, ancient Tamil merchant guilds had already established offices in South-East Asia. Chola and Pallava ships routinely traversed the Bay of Bengal to trade with China and the Far East.

Sawai Madho Singh II reading the British monarch's invitation

because of *kala pani* that many Indians were petrified of sea travel.

In 1901, Queen Victoria of Great Britain died. King Edward VII was named the next ruler of England *and* emperor of India. He invited some Indian maharajas for his coronation. One of these invitees was Maharaja Sawai Madho Singh II, the king of Jaipur. The maharaja was delighted by the invitation, but he faced a terrible dilemma. As an orthodox Hindu, he was prohibited from travelling overseas. And as the king, he was the defender of the faith in his kingdom. Could he be seen breaking the very laws he had sworn to protect?

Then there were the royal priests, who declared that he would invite divine wrath if he dared to travel overseas. Yet, this was a once-in-a-lifetime opportunity for him. Besides, how could he decline the invitation of the emperor of India himself?

So the maharaja assembled all his religious scholars and asked them for a solution. The scholars debated the matter and came up with a plan. It was decided that the king should not travel alone. The family deity would go along with him. Accordingly, the deity was ceremoniously lodged in the largest suite of the ship. The king himself took the second largest suite. Another large suite was reserved for the royal priest. He had to accompany the king to perform the daily rituals for the deity. The idea was to make it seem like neither of them had ever left their motherland. To further this illusion, soil collected from the city of Jaipur was spread thickly under the idol and under the king's bed.

The scholars also ordered that the ship used for the journey should be a 'pure' ship, meaning one that did not have beef cooked or served on it – ever. That was easily managed. The royal office simply asked the travel agency Thomas Cook to find a brand-new ship that had never sailed before. Although the solution was simple, it certainly didn't come cheap!

There was one more condition. The priests insisted that during the whole tour, which would take about three to four months, the maharaja was to drink water *only* from the River Ganga.

Luckily for them, they discovered three huge silver vats lying around in the palace treasury. Nobody remembered why they were made, but they fit the bill perfectly. They filled each vat with over 4,000 litres of water from the Ganga and loaded them on to the ship.

In 1902, the maharaja duly set sail on his purified ship with 132 servants, 600 pieces of luggage and King Edward's coronation gift, a glittering ceremonial sword. It wasn't all smooth sailing, though. The ship was caught in a violent storm near Aden in the Red Sea. The priests decided that the only way to appease the gods was to throw a silver vat overboard. By some strange coincidence, when they did so, the storm subsided! The maharaja reached London safely and attended the coronation. King Edward even visited the maharaja on his ship. The trip was a resounding success.

After they crushed the Great Indian Mutiny of 1857, the British exiled the rebels, including members of the Mughal clan, to Port Blair in the Andaman archipelago. The aim was both to isolate them from the Indian mainland, and also break them mentally. Since they had been made to cross the ocean for their exile (*kala pani*) they would lose their caste, and be ostracized by their own community; this punishment was considered worse than death. At first it was more of an open prison. But as more freedom fighters poured in, they built a high-security jail during 1896–1906, using prison labour. The prison itself came to be known as Kala Pani.

For a brief while the prison was captured by the Japanese and the Indian National Army (INA) during World War II. In a twist of fate, British officers and their Indian sympathizers were held in Kala Pani. Today it is a national monument dedicated to Indian freedom fighters.

The remaining two vats are now in the Jaipur Palace Museum. Each of them weighs a whopping 345 kilograms, and they are mentioned in the *Guinness World Records* as the world's largest silver artefacts.

This idea of travelling overseas with Ganga water was used at other times too. During World War I, it was the same idea that inspired the British and moved a million men. The British had a huge army of trained soldiers in India, but they faced an unexpected challenge when they had to move them to battlefronts abroad. The Indian soldiers refused to sail overseas! So the British simply loaded huge containers of Ganga water on board their ships, packed the Indian soldiers in and off they sailed around the globe. This idea was used in the coolie trade too, to transport cheap Indian labour to South Africa, Mauritius and other places.

So how is all this connected to the jail mentioned at the beginning of this chapter? This infamous Cellular Jail in Andaman was also called Kala Pani. In the early 1900s, this jail was used by the British to put away its most vocal political opponents. You had to cross an ocean to get to Andaman. So being imprisoned here meant not just jail time and torture, but something much worse: a loss of caste, a banishment from one's own community! That, to many, was a terrible punishment – much worse than imprisonment.

10

Yale's Madras Connection
ST MARY'S CHURCH, CHENNAI

> *He rose through the ranks in a very short span;*
> *He started as a clerk, but retired a wealthy man;*
> *This wheeler-dealer, through his illegal trades,*
> *Acquired a lot of power and money in spades;*
> *He traded in slaves, yet earned lasting fame –*
> *A reputed institution still goes by his name.*

Did you know that Yale University in Connecticut, USA, has the city of Madras to thank for its existence?

In 1639, the British East India Company established its first major Indian colony in Madras (now called Chennai). They built a fort called Fort St George close to the beach and consecrated the St Mary's Church inside it. The first ever wedding celebrated in the church was that of a Welshman named Elihu Yale. And his is an interesting story.

Twenty-one-year-old Yale joined the East India Company as a lowly clerk in 1671. He was a quick learner, but better still, he was able to make influential friends easily. Even as a junior officer, Yale was entrusted with crucial assignments. He proved excellent at wheeling and dealing, and rose through the ranks. By 1682, he was elected into the Governor's Council and by 1687, he had

St Mary's Church

Did you know that St Mary's Church in Madras is the oldest Anglican church, not just in India but in the entire eastern hemisphere? Over 300 years after it was built, it is still an active place of worship, and is the oldest continuously occupied British building in India. In the 17th century there weren't too many British engineers in India. So this church was designed by the master gunner of Fort St George. Given his artillery background, he designed the church with such thick walls and roofs that enemy cannonballs fired at it would bounce off. No wonder this church has survived so many attacks!

become the Governor of Madras. Eleven years later, he returned to London, a very wealthy and successful man. But this is not the happy story of a hard-working man. There is a dark side to him.

In those days, the East India Company had a rule that no British person could trade independently. Employees were expected to work full-time for the company and were not allowed to trade privately. Yale completely ignored this rule, and started buying and selling goods in his own name and made himself an enormous private fortune.

The directors of the East India Company were naturally unhappy with Yale's private trading. He was flouting their rules so openly that they could not afford to overlook it. So, in 1692, he was dismissed and charges were levelled against him.

But Yale wasn't particularly worried. He had influential friends in the Company. The two subsequent governors

Yale's governorship had another far-reaching consequence. He wielded so much power and flouted rules so openly that it made the board of directors of the East India Company rethink their administrative structures. In 1688, they decided to cut down the governor's absolute authority and hand over a part of it to a group of people instead – creating a corporation. Thus was born the Corporation of Madras in 1688. It is the second oldest civic corporation in the world, after London's.

of Madras were also good friends of his. So he calmly stayed on there and continued with his private trade.

In 1699, the directors found him not guilty and absolved him of all charges. Yale returned triumphantly to England – a multimillionaire. It is said he carried back five tonnes of merchandise with him! He settled down to a life of luxury in a posh locality in London. It was one small part of his ill-gotten wealth that made Yale immortal.

News of Yale's immense wealth spread as far as the United States. He was approached by a man named Cotton Mather from Connecticut, America. Mather was an administrator of the Connecticut College and he was looking for sponsors for his college. His father had been ousted from the management of Harvard, and so he was desperate to make his college more famous than Harvard. He approached Yale with a proposal: if Yale made a generous donation to the college, Mather would rename it after him. Yale's ego was touched. Perhaps he also thought this was a good way of purchasing respectability! He shipped some of his Indian loot to the United States, and the merchandise was auctioned off there. The sale fetched the college about GBP 800, a sizable sum in those days! The money was then used to construct a new building for the college, and the college was renamed after Yale. Today, we know it as the famous Yale University.

Cut to 2007 when Yale University was in the news for quietly removing a picture of Elihu Yale and replacing it with another. Why? The picture showed Yale and his friends being served by a dark boy, probably from Madras. A metallic collar around the boy's neck made it clear that he was not merely a servant, but a slave. The picture pointed to the darker story behind Yale's rise to riches.

When Yale was in India, he traded in textiles, gems and many other goods. But he also had a hand in the very ugly practice of slave trade.

In the 17th century, all colonial powers openly indulged in slave trade. They captured and sold people from their colonies as cheap labour to other countries. The East India Company was no exception. In the early days of this trade, petty criminals used to be sold as slaves. As time went on, even innocent children were kidnapped and sold off. Madras was a busy port, sending off Indian slaves to other British colonies. In fact, at one time there was a rule that every ship leaving the Madras port had to carry at least ten slaves! Yale, as the governor

Yale University

of Madras, officially conducted this business on behalf of the East India Company. But he also carried on the slave business privately and made much money for himself on the sly.

The lucrative slave trade from India came to an abrupt halt in 1689, when Mughal emperor Aurangzeb abolished slavery. The East India company was forced to stop the trade. But Yale did not. He ordered company ships to capture slaves from other places, like Madagascar, and kept the slave trade going.

Yale's ruthless treatment of people showed up in other areas as well. As the governor of Madras, Yale imposed very harsh punishments on Indians. They were rounded up even for small crimes and treated very cruelly. As you can imagine, Yale was not a popular governor. He flouted rules, set a bad example and did just as he pleased. Yet, he managed to amass a huge fortune and have an elite university named after him in Connecticut.

St Mary's Church in Chennai also remembers Yale with a prominent display of the wedding register that records Elihu Yale's wedding to Catherine Hynmer. Isn't it strange how, despite a life filled with terrible acts, one single donation brought eternal fame to Elihu Yale?

11

The Discovery of Ajanta
AJANTA CAVES, MAHARASHTRA

An Englishman went on a tiger hunt,
But stopped in his tracks when he saw up front
A U-shaped cliff with a waterfall
And a mysterious cave, behind that watery wall.
He walked inside and shone his torch around
And was dazzled by the paintings he found –
Red, green, blue, black, white and bold,
Buddhist paintings, over two thousand years old!
In the hills of Sahyadri, hidden in plain sight,
Lies this treasure trove – an artist's delight.

In 1819, in the jungles of the Waghora River Valley, near Aurangabad in Maharashtra, Captain John Smith of the 28th Madras Cavalry of the British East India Company was following tiger tracks. He was called 'Tiger' Smith, because he had shot not one or two tigers, but 99 of them in his career!

He hired a local shepherd as a guide and went into the jungle. Tiger hunting is illegal in modern India, but in those days it was a royal sport for maharajas and the higher ranks of the British in India. The Waghora River Valley, where the Sahyadri mountains rise above the Deccan Plateau, was home to many tigers. Soon the two of them reached a horseshoe shaped cliff from where the river cascaded down into a gorge. He found no tigers there, but his sharp eyes spotted a series of caves hidden behind the waterfall.

Smith was curious. He cleared the thick shrubs at the mouth of a cave and entered it. It was dark inside, so he lit up a torch made of dry leaves before heading in further. It was dusty and terribly smelly, and bats were flying all around. When his eyes adjusted to the dark, he found himself staring at something incredible: brilliant paintings and carvings of the Buddha, and of men, women, animals and trees – all coloured in the most vivid of hues. Captain Smith had discovered Cave 10 of the Ajanta Caves, as it is known today!

He was so astonished that he did something he shouldn't have. On one of the frescoes, he wrote 'John Smith, 28th Cavalry, 28th April, 1819', thereby becoming at once the discoverer *and* the first vandal of the Ajanta caves!

He returned to Madras, present-day Chennai, and dutifully reported this amazing find to his superiors. They in turn reported the find to the Bombay Literary Society and the Royal Asiatic Society. These were organizations set up by Englishmen who had a deep love for India and were interested in learning more about this vast land. Soon, many expeditions of soldiers and scholars went to visit Ajanta and the world got to know of the marvellous caves.

Ajanta painting

There are 30 caves in Ajanta, all carved between the second century BCE and the fourth century CE. That makes them over 2,000 years old! What exactly were these caves used for? Some caves were called *chaitya*s, meaning Buddhist worship halls, while others were called *vihara*s, meaning monasteries with hostels attached. All the caves

What are the Ajanta paintings about? They are mostly depictions of scenes from the Jataka tales, which are stories about the Buddha's previous lives. The style of the paintings, the costumes and scenes depicted, and the materials used, all give us insight into society two millennia ago. However, unless one understands the context of the painting, it is easy to be misled. For example, one painting in Cave 1, famously known as the 'Persian Embassy' was interpreted to be an image of the ambassador of Persian king Khosrow II presenting credentials to the Chalukya king Pulakeshin II. The Persian attire of some of the figures in the painting had completely fooled the early researchers and led to the wrong dating of the caves! It was only many decades later that another archaeologist proved that it was a scene from the Mahasudarsana Jataka tale! The painting actually depicts a king named Mahasudarsana holding court. In the Jataka tales, he was the king of Kushinagara; he was noble and generous and loved by his people. Moreover, he was the Buddha in a previous birth. What the earlier archaeologists had forgotten was that there was trade with the Sasanian Empire in those days, so it was not unusual to see 'Persian' looking men in a king's court!

Ajanta Caves

are filled with amazing sculptures and brightly coloured paintings. They tell us stories of an ancient time – stories of gods, people, society and customs.

But why were such beautiful paintings and carvings made in the middle of a jungle?

Two thousand years ago, this was no jungle. It was bang on the main trade route between the west coast and the Gangetic plains. In fact, even today the Mumbai–Delhi railway line passes very close to Ajanta. This fertile land in central India was ruled by a Hindu dynasty called the Satavahanas. Their kingdom was very strategically located and the empire stretched from coast to coast. So they traded with Rome, Arabia and Egypt on one side, and with China and the Far East on the other. They were right at the centre of the Indian subcontinent, so anyone going from north to south had to necessarily pass through Satavahana territory. Busy commercial towns sprang up all along the trade routes, and the Satavahanas earned huge revenue from taxes.

In those days, it was a tradition among Buddhists to maintain shelters all along trade routes. These shelters served as monasteries and inns for both merchants and Buddhist pilgrims. The Ajanta Caves were part of this tradition. These remarkable caves evolved during the reign of the Satavahanas. Their successors, the Vakatakas, who came to power in the third century CE, added another 24 new caves. One king in particular, Harisena, contributed significantly to Ajanta. Both the

The Satavahanas and Vakatakas were Hindu kings, but they respected Buddhism. In those days, both the kings and their subjects believed that sponsoring the making of caves like the ones at Ajanta would please the gods and give them a better life in their next birth. So it wasn't just King Harisena who donated money for these caves; his ministers, local headmen and even common people sponsored them as well. Visitors from afar used these caves as hostels and probably donated funds too. The famous Chinese explorers, Faxian and Xuanzang, have referred to these caves in their travelogues. Businessmen and monks continued to sponsor cave art even after the fall of the Vakatakas. After the eighth century CE, traffic declined and the jungle took over the caves.

Satavahanas and the Vakatakas had strong armies, which provided internal stability, and the bustling trade brought in much prosperity. This meant that the country was safe and rich, creating a comfortable environment for art to thrive.

After Harisena's death, this activity tapered off and Ajanta declined. By the end of the fifth century, Ajanta itself was no longer on the commercial route and the work on the caves came to a halt.

What is so great about Ajanta? To begin with, the artists must have been very determined to execute this project. In those days, there would have been no way to climb down the steep cliffside. So they would have hooked themselves to ropes and slowly descended about 100 feet down the cliff. Then they cut a letter-box-like slot into the cliff and continued to gingerly gouge out rocks to form a cave. The gouging must have been a delicate affair: they had to remove enough rock to make a cave, but leave back enough to support the roof and carve beautiful pillars. One mistake and the roof of the cave would have collapsed!

The artists themselves had to be highly skilled, with good knowledge of Buddhist lore. The natural colours that they used for the paintings would fade if exposed to sunlight and moisture. So they had to paint in semi-darkness. Since there wasn't much light inside the caves, the artists would have used white cloth screens or filled the depressions in the caves with water. This provided them with reflected sunlight. Straining their eyes to the

After a glorious 2,000 years, Ajanta is under serious threat. The paintings are deteriorating due to centuries of moisture seepage, and exposure to the vagaries of temperature and light. Many early attempts to 'save' the monument caused more damage because the conservation techniques used were primitive. There is a chance that these murals may completely fade within a hundred years. In recent years, the Archaeological Survey of India (ASI) has devised non-destructive methods of conservation that include digital copying and reconstruction of images without touching the original. Scientists are in a race against time in a last-ditch effort to protect this heritage before it completely fades away.

utmost, they must have mixed six basic natural colours to produce the beautiful paintings. It was work that demanded *extreme* patience and skill.

Today, Ajanta is a UNESCO World Heritage site. It teems with tourists, delighting in the beauty of the artwork it shelters. And Captain 'Tiger' Smith is best known for the tiger he *did not* shoot!

12

The Misadventures of Vasco da Gama
ST FRANCIS CHURCH, KOCHI

A petty Portuguese nobleman, with a terrible temper to boot,
Was chosen to lead an expedition and discover a new
sea route;
Not the best diplomat, he ruffled feathers wherever he went,
But in court politics he excelled, and so he got sent
On an adventurous journey that he bungled his way through,
Though he messed up his chances, he got way more than his due.

Who was the first European to come to India?

If you thought it was Vasco da Gama, think again! He was not even the first Portuguese individual to come to India. The Greek conqueror Alexander of Macedonia came to India by land around 326 BCE. As early as the first century CE, Roman and Greek merchants were regularly visiting India through the Arabian Sea. Goods from India went across the Arabian Sea, via what was called the old Roman route – from the Red Sea and through the Ottoman Empire – to reach Europe.

The Ottoman Empire, also called the Turkish Empire, was a powerful Islamic kingdom in the 1500s. It controlled the trade route to India and levied high taxes on European merchants who travelled through their empire. Naturally, this pushed up prices of goods sold in Europe. Portugal and Spain, the two most powerful countries in Europe at that time, desperately wanted to break this Ottoman monopoly over trade with India.

So Spain sent out explorers and one of them was Christopher Columbus. He set off to find a route to the east, but he ended up discovering America.

The Portuguese too sent explorers out to discover sea routes to the east, and one of them was Vasco da Gama. History credits him with discovering a new sea route to India. But did he really deserve this credit? Let's look at what he achieved. And what he did not.

In 1488, ten years before Vasco reached India, another Portuguese explorer named Bartolomeu Dias managed to sail around the Cape of Good Hope at the southern tip of Africa. This discovery meant that it was theoretically possible to sail all the way to India by a new sea route, one that completely bypassed the Middle East.

King Manuel I of Portugal was very excited by this possibility. If the new sea route was established, Portugal could become rich by making trade deals with Indian kings. He chose Vasco da Gama for this mission. Vasco was a petty nobleman from Lisbon, known for his arrogance and violent temper – hardly the kind to lead diplomatic missions. He wasn't a great sailor either.

Yet, King Manuel I appointed him head of the first Indian Armada. So why was he chosen? Vasco was very good at court politics and managed to pull all the right

Vasco da Gama

strings. Luckily for him, earlier Portuguese scouting missions had already gathered a lot of information about sea routes to Kerala. And for a part of the route, he was accompanied by Bartolomeu Dias himself, the man who had discovered the sea route around Africa. Vasco's task was therefore a relatively simple one. He had to sail across the Arabian Sea, befriend the local Indian kings and coax trading agreements out of them. It required tact and wisdom. Vasco had neither, and he failed spectacularly.

Vasco set sail from Lisbon with four ships and 170 men. His misadventures began almost as soon as he left port. He tried to get concessions from the Sultan of Mozambique by pretending he was a Muslim. His bluff was discovered, and he barely escaped with his life. Then he unexpectedly

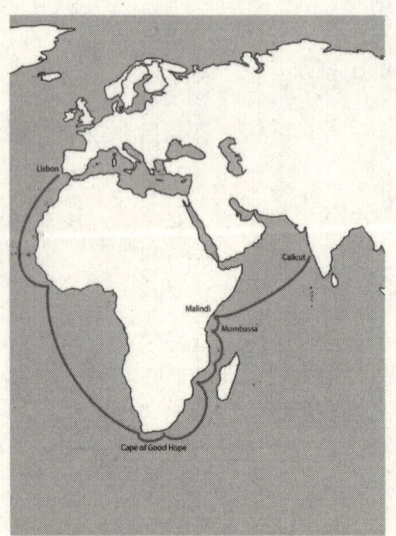

Vasco da Gama's sea route to India

resorted to random piracy at Mombasa and was chased away. Finally, he landed in India in 1498, in a place called Kappadu, in Kozhikode (also called Calicut). At that time, the rich Kozhikode kingdom was ruled by a powerful dynasty called Samuthiri. It would have been sensible for Vasco to humbly approach the king and develop a relationship. But no, Vasco first insulted him by offering cheap trinkets as gifts. Then he demanded monopoly rights to trade in Kozhikode. The king was outraged. Why would the Samuthiri entertain an unknown Portuguese who had nothing to offer in return? He refused!

Vasco was furious. In a fit of rage, he kidnapped some locals, and tried to make a break for it. The Kozhikode army nearly caught him, but he quickly got into his ship and sailed away. But the timing of that exit was sheer madness. Vasco had forgotten that the monsoons were seasonal. The journey that had taken 23 days on their way to India, took 132 days during their return. By the time Vasco reached home, he had lost two ships and more than 100 men.

A weary Vasco reached Lisbon, a complete failure, with no trading contract from any Indian King. But he had a shipload of spices. And these spices were worth more than 60 times the cost of the expedition. So he received a hero's welcome. King Manuel made him a Lord, and later even gave him a pompous title – 'Admiral of the Seas of Arabia, Persia, India and all Orient'. But he quietly made certain that Vasco was not sent on the next voyage.

Pedro Alvares Cabral belonged to a noble family in Portugal. In 1500 CE, he was appointed the commander-in-chief of the fleet sailing to India. Vasco da Gama's first voyage had already established the sea route to India along the African coast. But Cabral did something different. After crossing the Canary Islands, he sailed west. Within a month, he landed in mainland Brazil in South America. Cabral knew he had discovered an important place. He erected a huge cross and claimed Brazil for Portugal. Then he sailed on to India. When he returned to Lisbon, he carried back a large supply of spices yielding 800 per cent profit to the king. This far exceeded Vasco's achievement. Cabral claimed a new country in South America and established a trading station in India. And, yet, Portugal treated him badly. When Portugal decided to send a 'revenge' fleet to attack the Samuthiri, Cabral was named as the commander. But Vasco's manipulations ensured that he was sidelined, and Vasco became the commander. Cabral never got the king's favour after that. He retired to a small town on a royal pension, and died in 1520, a completely forgotten hero.

Instead, he sent Pedro Alvares Cabral to India. Cabral was a good leader. He tried to repair the relationship with the Samuthiri king in Kozhikode. But the ill will created by Vasco was not yet forgotten. The Samuthiri chased Cabral's fleet out of Kozhikode. So he went to the Samuthiri's rival, the king of Kochi, and established a profitable trade relationship with him. With that, the Portuguese finally got a toehold to establish a settlement in Kochi. Cabral too returned with huge quantities of spices, and his expedition was a major commercial success.

Meanwhile, Vasco was itching to go to India again. In 1502, he convinced King Manuel that he was the right person to lead a revenge fleet against the Kozhikode Samuthiri. But instead of getting the best sailors in his crew, Vasco appointed his family members to key posts in the fleet. The ship's crew included two of Vasco's uncles, two brothers-in-law and one nephew.

When Vasco reached Kozhikode, the Samuthiri was quite willing to reconsider a treaty with the Portuguese. But once again Vasco spoilt chances of peace with his brash behaviour. His fleet surrounded Kozhikode, and attacked and looted unarmed merchant vessels. They cut off the ears and noses of the captured crew. But the Samuthiri held out. So the only thing Vasco could do was to go back to Kochi, load up his ships with spices and head home.

On the way back, Vasco decided to play pirate. He spotted a ship carrying over 400 Muslim pilgrims on their way to the holy city of Mecca. Vasco's men boarded the ship and plundered all valuables on-board. Then he locked up all the passengers in the ship and set fire to it.

King Manuel had had enough of Vasco. He quietly sidelined him from his court. But Vasco, being Vasco, promptly blackmailed the king by threatening to defect to Spain, Portugal's sworn enemy. So the king made Vasco the count of a faraway province and silenced him for the next two decades.

Vasco was not done yet, though. When King Manuel died, he cozied up to the new king, John III, and in 1524, he returned to India as a viceroy, the highest post in Portuguese India. But within three months of his arrival, he died of malaria in Kochi. He was buried at the St Francis Church in Kochi. You can still see the gravestone inside the church. Vasco's body was later dug up by his son and re-buried in Lisbon.

Thus ended the career of a man who is hailed as a famous pioneer, but whose dark past included botched attempts at setting up a colony, plain butchery and acts

The St Francis Church is where Vasco's mortal remains were buried in 1524. It stayed there for 14 years, until Vasco's son facilitated the transfer of the remains to Portugal.

The church was first built in 1516 by Franciscan monks who dedicated it to St Anthony. In 1663, the Dutch drove the Portuguese out of Kochi. They took over the Catholic church from the Portuguese. What do you think they did with it? They filled it up with gunpowder! At first, they wanted to destroy it. But then they had second thoughts and did not light the fuse. The church survived and was converted into a Protestant church. Then in 1795 the British drove the Dutch out of Kochi. They took control of the city, and eventually took over this church too. The British were Anglicans, and so in 1804, the church began life afresh again – this time as an Anglican church. So at different points in its life, the church has been Catholic, Protestant and Anglican!

Many famous explorers were infamous for switching loyalties between kings. All they wanted was someone to sponsor their voyages and believe in their dreams. Take the case of Ferdinand Magellan. He was a Portuguese navigator and explorer who sailed under the sponsorship of both Portugal and Spain. King Manuel I of Portugal was his initial sponsor. Unfortunately, the relationship between the two soured and Magellan finally offered his services to the king of Spain, Charles I, who was only too happy to poach this daring sailor from his sworn enemy. This was considered a treacherous act by the Portuguese, and Magellan never returned to Portugal. In 1519, he led an expedition funded by King Charles that travelled west from Spain to reach the eastern lands of Asia. King Manuel went out of his way to sabotage the expedition. But fortunately for Magellan, he sailed away successfully. Although he was killed before the expedition ended, two of his ships successfully circumnavigated the earth for the first time and returned to Spain in 1522, bringing immense credit to King Charles I.

of piracy. However, he deserves credit for being the first sea captain from Europe to reach India by sailing around Africa. From a Portuguese point of view, he laid the foundation for the Portuguese colonization of India and Asia. More significantly, the sea route that he discovered remained the most important trade route for the next 400-odd years. The opening of the Suez Canal in 1869 changed that. Even today, supertankers that cannot squeeze through the Suez Canal take Vasco's route!

13

The Curse of the Koh-i-noor

RED FORT, DELHI

It was the centrepiece of an exquisite throne
That cost twice as much as the Taj;
This huge diamond, the size of a hen's egg,
Was carted away during the British Raj.
A mountain of light, it literally means,
It carries a curse that affects kings, but not queens.

The British East India Company came to India to trade in such ordinary things as cotton, tobacco and spices. Sometimes, through a stroke of sheer good luck, they chanced upon priceless historical objects like the Amaravati marbles or the seals from Mohenjo-daro. Sometimes, through clever manipulation, they got their hands on brilliant, sparkly things – gems, jewels and precious objects. A good number of these quietly went into the private estates of the employees of the East India Company.

Many more went straight to the British Crown. Let's talk about the sparkliest of all the treasures that left India: the Peacock Throne, a solid gold throne made for the Mughal emperor Shah Jahan. It was richly set with hundreds of precious stones, one of which was

Peacock Throne

the fabled Koh-i-noor diamond. 'Koh-i-noor' literally means 'mountain of light'.

Shah Jahan ruled over an extremely prosperous kingdom. He ruled at a time when the Mughal Empire was at its peak and was the richest kingdom in the world. Shah Jahan built many beautiful monuments, including the stately Red Fort. This fort was Shah

> **Was the Red Fort always red?**
> The Red fort was completed in 1648. The city of
> Shahjahanabad that came up around it became the new
> Mughal capital, and it soon housed over two million people!
> That is more than twice the combined population of London
> and Paris of the time! The outer walls and ramparts of the fort
> were red, because they were made of brick and sandstone.
> There were marble buildings inside the fort which were, of
> course, all white. Some of the buildings inside were plastered
> over with white lime plaster, giving them the smooth feel
> of marble. A few of them were gilded with gold too. But
> over time, the plaster crumbled, exposing the red bricks
> underneath. Later Mughal kings did not have money for its
> upkeep, so it became almost all red. What we see now is
> perhaps only one-third of the original Red Fort complex.
> Today it is a UNESCO World Heritage monument.

Jahan's residence. It was also his royal court where he
would meet his subjects and listen to their grievances.
As a king, Shah Jahan wanted to project an aura of might
and invincibility. So he commissioned a magnificent
throne – the 'Takht-e-Taus' or the 'Peacock Throne'. It
is estimated that he spent twice as much on the Peacock
Throne as he did on the Taj Mahal.

Written records tell us that the Peacock Throne
used up over 1,100 kilograms of solid gold! It was
studded with another 230 kilograms of precious stones
– diamonds, rubies, sapphires, emeralds and more. The
throne had a richly enamelled canopy supported by 12

pillars. Each pillar was decorated with a pair of peacocks, inlaid with gems, hence the name. The gems on the throne included some of the most famous stones known at that time: the Timur ruby, a soft pink diamond called the Daria-i-Noor, and at the very top, a massive, clear diamond called the Koh-i-Noor. On this spectacular throne sat Shah Jahan and his successors, showing off their might and power to a bedazzled world!

What did the Peacock Throne really look like? We do not know. Much has been written about it, by both Indian chroniclers and European travellers of the Shah Jahan era. But the accounts are sometimes contradictory, because no one really dared to come close to the emperor, and everyone saw it only from a respectable distance. There are no contemporary paintings of the throne either.

But behind that razzle-dazzle lay gory power struggles; brother blinded brother, and uncles and nephews killed each other mercilessly. Shah Jahan himself was imprisoned by his own son, and remained helpless as his sons murdered each other for his throne. And from its vantage point on the Peacock Throne, the Koh-i-noor saw it all – the beginning of the end of the Mughal Empire.

As generations passed, there was a decline in the power of the Mughal kings. In 1739, something terrible happened in Delhi. Muhammad Shah, the Mughal emperor then, was a very weak king. It was the ideal opportunity for the Persian king Nadir Shah to invade Delhi. Nadir Shah barrelled his way in, killing and looting ruthlessly. He massacred over 30,000 people in just one day, and plundered everything of value, including the Peacock Throne. He pulled out the Koh-i-noor diamond and the Timur Ruby from the throne and proudly wore them on his arm band. As for the throne, it was never seen again – it was probably melted down for its gold value.

What happened to the Koh-i-noor? Today, it sits snugly in the crown that Queen Elizabeth I wore at her coronation. Even today, visitors to the Tower of London are dazzled by the massive diamond lodged in the crown on display there. But this diamond has a bloodstained past and has been through a wild journey across kingdoms and continents. Almost every time, its owner either lost power or died an untimely death. The Koh-i-noor, they say, is a cursed stone.

What happened to the other gems on the Peacock Throne? While the Peacock Throne itself is lost forever, some of the other precious stones on the throne have survived. The Daria-i-noor is now a part of the Iranian crown jewels. Some of the gems that were looted have been traced to other parts of the world, including Russia and Turkey.

The origin of this jewel is shrouded in mystery. It is believed to have been mined in the 11th century, from

Crown of Queen Elizabeth I

the Kollur pits of the Golconda mines, in present-day Andhra Pradesh. Did you know that until the 1700s, there were no diamond mines anywhere in the world except India? The Golconda mines were the only diamond mines in the whole world. In those days, the Golconda area (present-day Andhra Pradesh and Telangana) was under the control of a dynasty called the Kakatiyas, and they were the first to own this diamond. In 1310 CE, the Kakatiya kings were defeated by the army of a Delhi sultan, Ala-ud-din Khilji, and the Kakatiya dynasty itself ended soon after. The Koh-i-noor was part of the loot that went to the Delhi sultan.

In 1526, the first Mughal king, Babur, conquered Delhi, and the diamond became his. His son, Humayun, inherited it, but soon ended up losing his kingdom. He eventually regained the throne, but died in a freak accident barely six months later. His great-grandson was Shah Jahan, who had it set in the Peacock Throne. And then Nadir Shah carted it away. So how did it make its way to the British crown?

In 1747, a few years after he got hold of the Koh-i-noor, Nadir Shah met with a gruesome death, and the Persian Empire itself began to break up.

The diamond then fell into the hands of a close confidant of Nadir Shah, an Afghan general named Ahmad Shah Durrani. He took this bauble of bad luck with him to Afghanistan, where he established his own independent kingdom.

After Durrani's death, there was a vicious fight for his throne. The Koh-i-noor passed through many hands during this time, and witnessed a savage spree of killing, poisoning and blinding. Eventually, it reached a prince named Shah Shuja Durrani. He too lost his throne and had to flee to Lahore in present-day Pakistan in 1813.

Lahore was the capital of Maharaja Ranjit Singh, ruler of the prosperous Sikh Empire. The maharaja agreed to give Shah Shuja Durrani refuge, in exchange for the Koh-i-noor. It is said that Ranjit Singh wanted to donate the diamond to the Jagannath Temple in Puri, but he died before he could act on his wish. Soon after, the Sikh Empire itself started disintegrating.

This was just the opportunity the British in India were looking for. Punjab was rich and strategically important. Now, it was without a powerful king. They quietly manipulated the turn of events, and soon took Punjab and all its crown jewels for themselves.

The thrilled British Viceroy of India decided to gift the Koh-i-noor to Queen Victoria. He arranged for a ship to transport the diamond to London. But they say the curse sailed with it. There was an outbreak of cholera on board. Then the ship ran into a violent gale, which it barely survived. But the diamond finally managed to reach London.

In 1850, Maharaja Ranjeet Singh's son, 10-year-old prince Duleep was made to ceremonially hand over the Koh-i-noor to the Queen. It was decided that the diamond would be fixed to her crown. But it was way too heavy. And people felt it was not sparkly enough for the queen's crown.

So a decision was made to cut more facets into it. That is how the 191-carat Koh-i-noor became a 105-carat diamond. But even after that cut, the Koh-i-noor is still one of the largest diamonds in the world.

The Koh-i-noor has seen the end of powerful dynasties – across India, Pakistan, Afghanistan and Persia. Is it any surprise that it acquired a reputation of being cursed? Strangely enough, the curse is said to affect only men and not women! Till date only the British queens have worn the diamond on their crowns, never a king!

Should Britain return the Koh-i-noor to India? The Indian government has made the demand several times, insisting that it was acquired through unfair means. Pakistan also has staked a claim on it because Maharaja Ranjit Singh ruled from Lahore, which is now in Pakistan. And the Afghans believe the Koh-i-noor belongs to them because Shah Shuja Durrani surrendered it to Maharaja Ranjit Singh under duress. The British remain unfazed. To them, the Koh-i-noor, cursed or not, is still their prized possession – the jewel in their crown.

14

The Quest for the Pandya Crown Jewels

MEENAKSHI TEMPLE, MADURAI

In the heart of Madurai an ancient temple stands tall;
It has seen mighty kingdoms rise, and eventually fall,
But for many centuries one dynasty stood strong
And tussled with another that ruled for nearly as long;
Kings went down fighting, crown jewels changed hands,
Until came a king who crowned himself 'the emperor of
three lands'.

In the heart of the old city of Madurai lies an ancient temple dedicated to Goddess Meenakshi. It is not known when it was first built, but the core of the temple has been held sacred for ages. It finds mention in the Sangam literature – that is, ancient Tamil literature dating back to the third century BCE. So one can assume that it has been a sacred spot for at least 2,000 years.

The temple we see today was largely built by the Nayak rulers of the 16th century. But one of the *gopurams* or entrance towers is believed to have been built as early as 1216 CE by a Pandya king named Maravarman Sundara Pandyan I. For centuries, Madurai was the capital of the Pandya kingdom.

Just how old is the Meenakshi temple? Well, all we can say is that it is genuinely ancient. Sangam literature, composed between the third century BCE and third century CE, mentions the temple, dating it to over 2,000 years ago. Not quite like it is today, perhaps, but the spot in the centre of Madurai was considered holy that far back. Around the seventh century, there was a group of ardent Shiva devotees called the Nayanmars. They were great composers of poems, and they have sung praises of the temple. So we have definitive historic evidence for that period. The temple in its current form must have existed from the 12th century. The oldest surviving portions are the Meenakshi and Sundareswarar shrines well inside the temple complex along with the *gopuram*, the entrance tower to the Sundareswarar shrine. This shrine is dedicated to Shiva: Sundareswarar is another name of Shiva, literally meaning 'Handsome Lord'. These are said to have been built by Jatavarman Kulasekhara Pandyan – a king who ruled Madurai as a vassal of the Cholas between 1190 and 1216. The impressive eastern *gopuram* was probably built by Maravarman Sundara Pandyan I who ruled Madurai between 1216–1238. In 1311, the temple was nearly razed by the armies of the Delhi Sultanate led by their general Malik Kafur. In the 16th century, it was reconstructed by the Vijayanagara and Nayak kings.

Who exactly were the Pandyas? They were one of the longest ruling dynasties in India, and reigned over large parts of the south. The Pandyas, too, find mention in Sangam literature. A poem from the second century BCE, titled 'Madurai Kanchi', speaks of a large and lavish

Meenakshi Temple

city, whose streets were filled with flower sellers and their fragrant ware, jewellers selling pearls and precious stones, and grain merchants with sacks of pepper and heaps of grain. The Pandyas are also mentioned in the Greek and Roman records of the time. The last of the Pandya kings ruled in the 14th century. That's a reign of nearly 1,700 years for the dynasty!

While there are historical records of these later Pandyas, the further one goes back in time, the harder it gets to separate history from myth and legend. So in this story too, we will be going back and forth between popular legend and recorded history.

In fact, the Pandyas believed that they were descendants of Goddess Meenakshi herself. The ancient epic, the Mahabharata, refers to a king named Malayadhwaja Pandyan from Madurai, who is said to have supported the Pandavas and helped them win the Kurukshetra war. Legend goes that this king prayed for a child and was blessed with a daughter, Meenakshi.

He brought her up as a warrior princess and she conquered all lands right up to the Himalayas. But at Mount Kailash, she fell in love with Shiva and married him. This divine couple ruled over Madurai for many years. Their son was named Ugra Kumara Pandya. From him, it is said, was born the dynasty of the Pandyas.

Historically, the Pandyas were one of the oldest south Indian dynasties. There were two other dynasties in south India that also ruled at the same time, and for nearly as long: the Cheras, who ruled over present-day Kerala, and the Cholas, who ruled from Thanjavur in Tamil Nadu. For over 1,000 years, the southern peninsula saw many squabbles, skirmishes and pitched battles amongst the kings of these dynasties, as each tried hard to dominate the other two. Sometimes, the Sri Lankan kings, who were just a stone's throw away, were also drawn into these wars. Not surprisingly, the earliest record of this power struggle also comes from mythology.

Legend says that at one time, south India was ravaged by a drought. All the three great kings of the south travelled to heaven and met Indra, the king of heavens and the god of rain, to ask for relief. The Chera and the Chola kings took a seat below Indra's and humbly requested for rain. On the other hand, Ugra Pandya, the son of Shiva and Meenakshi, sat next to him like an equal and demanded rain. Indra was impressed by the young man's confidence and presented him with a beautiful necklace called the Indra-Aaram. But he was also a little peeved by his brashness. So he sent rains to the Chola and Chera kingdoms, but withheld the rain clouds from Pandya land. Ugra was furious and went to war with Indra. With the divine weapons he had inherited from his father, Shiva, he defeated Indra and secured bountiful rains for his kingdom. Ugra wore the Indra-Aaram forever after, as a symbol of his power and his divine origins. And so did all the later Pandya kings.

But did the Indra-Aaram really exist?

The ancient Tamil epic *Silappadikaram*, dated between the third and seventh centuries CE, talks of the Pandya kings wearing a beautifully crafted necklace called the Indra–Aaram. The Pandya craftsmen were known for their skill in making pearl and gold jewellery. The best specimens must have been made for the kings. It is plausible that the Pandya kings themselves carefully cultivated such myths to project an aura of invincible power. The Indra–Aaram became the most precious heirloom of the Pandya kings and a symbol of royal power.

In 910 CE, the Chola King Parantaka I defeated the Pandya King Rajasimha II. The defeated Pandya ruler fled to Sri Lanka with all his crown jewels. Later, he secretly escaped to the Chera country, because his mother happened to be a Chera princess. But he left behind his crown jewels in Sri Lanka for safekeeping.

The victorious Chola king, Parantaka I, occupied the Pandya capital, Madurai, and assumed the title 'Madurai Kondan', meaning 'the conqueror of Madurai'. But it was a pyrrhic victory, because he had no crown jewels to show for it. It must have rankled because towards the end of his reign, he decided to make one more attempt to acquire the Pandya crown jewels. He wrote to the new king of Sri Lanka demanding their return. The Sri Lankan king refused. So Parantaka invaded that island, forcing the Sri Lankan king to flee to the hills of Ruhunu. But the Sri Lankan king took the Pandya jewels with him, and a frustrated Parantaka had to return empty-handed.

Three generations later, in 985 CE, Parantaka's great-grandson, Rajaraja Chola, the king who built the gigantic Brihadeeswara Temple in Thanjavur, attacked Sri Lanka and captured the northern part. Once again, the Sri Lankan king fled to Ruhunu hills, and once again, the Chola king had to return without the crown jewels!

Finally, Rajaraja's son, Rajendra Chola, who built the beautiful Gangaikonda Cholapuram Temple, succeeded in the mission that had eluded his father and his great-great-grandfather. In 1017 CE, he defeated the Sri Lankan king and made that island a Chola province. The Sri Lankan king was taken prisoner, and the Pandya crown jewels, including the divine Indra-Aaram, finally became a part of the Chola treasury. With that, Rajendra Chola took on the title of 'Mummudi Chola', meaning 'Emperor of three kingdoms': Pandya, Chera and Chola.

The Indra-Aaram stayed with the Cholas for the next 250 years. In 1279, the Cholas were defeated by the Pandyas. But the victory was short-lived, for very soon, the Pandyas lost everything to the Delhi Sultans who attacked Madurai in the early 14th century. It was during this attack that the older structure of the Meenakshi Temple was almost completely destroyed. It was also during those turbulent times that the Pandya crown jewels, including the Indra-Aaram, were lost forever.

Still, the Pandya–Meenakshi legacy lives on in Madurai. To this day, one of the most common names for boys in Madurai is Pandyan, and Meenakshi continues to be a popular name for girls – a nod to a dynasty that ruled over these parts for over 17 centuries.

Though the Pandyas ruled for such a long time, unfortunately there are hardly any Pandya monuments in Madurai today. Near the eastern *gopuram* of the Meenakshi temple is a section of the old Pandya fort, a nondescript gateway called the 'Vittavaasal'. The fort itself has been completely torn down or buried under, and this is the only portion that still stands. 'Vittavaasal' literally means 'the gateway that got left behind'.

The city of Madurai was fortified by both the Pandya kings and the Nayak kings. The old Pandya fort existed until the 16th century, when the Nayak kings brought it down and built their own fort. The Nayak fort was brought down in the 19th century, interestingly, by the residents of Madurai. In 1801, Madurai fell into the hands of the British East India Company. At that time, the Nayak fort and the moat around it were still intact. But the population of Madurai was growing rapidly and the British decided to bring down the fort walls to allow the city to expand. However, instead of spending their own money to get the work done, the British collector of the time, John Blackburne, and his assistant, Marret, decided to entice local residents to do the work for them. They announced that anyone could come and break down the fort and use the rubble to fill up the moat. And that space would then belong to the person who had filled it up. In a very short span of time there was neither a fort nor a moat, but a brand new street and many new landowners. This street, which was once a moat, is now ironically called Marret Street, in honour of a man who pulled down a piece of Madurai's history.

15

A Divine Wedding That United a Town

THIRUMALAI NAYAK PALACE, MADURAI

It was the wedding of the goddess, the queen of this town –
From his home atop a hill, the bride's brother came down,
But he took his time, made leisurely stops and turned up
too late –
He missed the wedding, and so marched right back, miffed
and irate;
It's a story that to this day the entire town celebrates –
Colourfully decked chariots are the highlight of this yearly fete.

For nearly every visitor to Madurai, the towering Meenakshi Temple located right in the middle of the old city is a must-see. After all, this goddess is considered the queen of Madurai. But there is also a palace nearby, which draws a large number of visitors – a palace that is not as imposing as Queen Meenakshi's temple, but elegant in its own right. The Thirumalai Nayak Palace bears testimony to a king who took Madurai to great heights.

King Thirumalai Nayak has left his mark in many ways on the history of Madurai. He left behind many

Thirumalai Nayak (r. 1623–59 CE) was undoubtedly the greatest of the Nayak kings. His reign was relatively peaceful, and it was a time when Madurai grew in size and splendour. In the 1630s, the king decided to build a palace to commemorate his rule. But not just any palace. Thirumalai Nayak was determined to build a palace unlike any other in the south! He selected an area in the heart of Madurai and poured a vast sum of money into the project. The Thirumalai Nayak Palace was completed in 1636, and it was every bit as grand as he intended.

It is a fusion of architectural styles. Many of its features are Indo–Saracenic, meaning a mix of Hindu, Muslim and Gothic architectural styles. Its huge pillars reflect the German Gothic style. Add high ceilings, graceful arches and generous proportions, and you have a palace that in its heyday would have taken one's breath away. There was a large durbar hall, a pavilion for the family, prayer rooms and a harem, and a theatre where dance and music was performed. There was also an armoury, a temple, a sports yard and a pool. Today, barely a fourth of the enormous building remains.

So what happened to all those structures? In 1665, Chokkanatha Nayak, the grandson of Thirumalai Nayak, decided to shift his capital to Tiruchirappalli, which lies to the north of Madurai. He dismantled large parts of the palace and carted them back with him – to be used in his new palace. The old palace was left unused, and gradually it started falling apart. In recent times, it has been taken over by the ASI and renovated. A visit to the 'Mahal', as the locals call it, can still give you a small glimpse of its former grandeur.

Thirumalai Nayak Palace

monuments, but more interestingly, a tradition that he introduced 400 years ago still remains one of the biggest draws of the city. In the Tamil month of Chithirai, which falls between April and May in the Gregorian calendar, Madurai goes into festival mode. The city comes alive to celebrate the annual Chithirai festival that lasts for over two weeks, bringing together people of all classes and even uniting followers of different gods. And Thirumalai Nayak is said to be the man who started it all.

Who was Thirumalai Nayak? Madurai has always been closely associated with two dynasties, the Pandyas and the Nayaks – in that order. By the 14th century, the power of the long ruling Pandyas had come to an end, and large parts of southern India were taken over by the Vijayanagara Empire, which had its capital in Hampi, in modern-day Karnataka. Madurai too was annexed to this powerful empire, and the Vijayanagara kings appointed governors, called Nayaks, to rule over it.

In the early 1500s, a Vijayanagara general named Nagama Nayak, who was then the governor of Madurai, broke away from the king and asserted his independence. The furious king, Krishnadevaraya, branded him a traitor and sent a general named Visvanatha Nayak to capture him. Visvanatha was successful, and he brought Nagama back in chains to Vijayanagara. The king promptly rewarded Visvanatha Nayak by making him the new governor of Madurai.

What happened to Nagama Nayak? He was pardoned and set free. Visvanatha was Nagama Nayak's son. He pleaded with the king for his father's life and the king graciously agreed.

Visvanatha Nayak ruled Madurai well. Towards the end of his rule, the Vijayanagara Empire itself started disintegrating. Eventually, Madurai became an independent kingdom under the rule of the Nayak kings.

The Nayak dynasty of Madurai consisted of 13 rulers, who reigned for over 200 years. Thirumalai Nayak ruled between 1623 and 1659. In that period, he made Madurai a vibrant and bustling city, famous for its trade, industry, architecture, culture and of course, the Chithirai festival.

As mentioned before, legend has it that Meenakshi, the all-powerful goddess, was the queen of Madurai. Her consort is none other than Lord Shiva. Their wedding is believed to have taken place in Madurai, and it is said that it was a grand affair, attended by all the gods. The guest of honour was Lord Vishnu, the Protector. He was considered goddess Meenakshi's brother, and so he was given the honour of giving away the bride.

Just 20 kilometres away from Madurai is a hill range with a temple on it; the hill is called Azhagar Kovil, home to Lord Vishnu. And it is from this temple that Lord Vishnu is said to have begun his journey to Madurai, to attend his sister's marriage. But he took his own sweet time, stopping at many places along the way, meeting devotees and accepting their offerings. By the time he reached the banks of the river Vaigai, which flows through the city, the wedding ceremony was already over. Vishnu was shocked. He magnanimously handed over the wedding gifts he had carried with him, but refused to enter Madurai. In a fine fit of fury, he turned around and headed right back to the Azhagar Hills.

Azhagar Kovil

Like many south Indian temples, the Azhagar Kovil too has a hoary past. Its exact age is not clear, but it finds mention in ancient Tamil Sangam literature (roughly third century BCE–third century CE). There is a rather pretty verse which urges everyone to visit this temple with family and friends while one is still young, so as to enjoy Vishnu's blessings for long. The temple also finds mention in the *Silappadikaram*, one of the five grand epics of Tamil literature, composed probably between the third and seventh centuries CE. Later, during the eight–ninth centuries CE, the Alwars, who were Vaishnavite saints, sang praises of this temple.

These works have been collected and are sung even today. The structure we see today may not be quite that old. The fort walls that surround the temple are believed to have been built by Pandya kings. The earliest evidence of Pandya contribution relates to a king named Jatavarman Sundara Pandyan, who ruled in the 1200s. He gold-plated the tower over the sanctum. Later, the Cholas, the Vijayanagara kings and the Nayak kings all added to the temple. Thirumalai Nayak, in particular, is credited with much renovation work in the temple. The temple has many rare Vijayanagara-era sculptures.

How is this story connected to Thirumalai Nayak? Historians believe that this story is entirely made up, by none other than King Thirumalai Nayak himself. During his reign, the Shaivites (worshippers of Shiva) celebrated a temple festival in April every year, marking Meenakshi's wedding to Shiva. The Vaishnavites (worshippers of Vishnu) had their own festival that they celebrated between January and February of every year. These two religious groups rarely saw eye to eye.

Thirumalai Nayak himself was a devout Hindu who respected both the Shaivite and Vaishnavite traditions, and believed in the unity of faith. To broker peace between the two sects, he decided to combine the Meenakshi marriage festival and the Azhagar Kovil festival into one bigger, grander festival. He consulted scholars and used Hindu folklore to come up with a story that sounded credible. Vishnu was identified as Meenakshi's brother and assigned the all-important task of giving the bride away.

What did Thirumalai achieve with this new narrative? He created the impression that the two gods – Shiva and Vishnu – were related by marriage, so that there would be no cause for animosity between their followers. In one stroke, he had united the Shaivites and Vaishnavites, and ensured peace. He achieved an economic goal too. The earlier festivals, which fell during busy periods of a farmer's calendar, required them to take time off from farming during the festivals. This reduced agricultural productivity which in turn reduced revenues of the state. The month of Chithirai, during which the combined festival is celebrated, is the slack season for agricultural labour. Farmers could now enjoy the festivities without worrying about the harvest! Also, the rural and the urban sections of the population met and mingled, bringing people of his kingdom closer. This annual gala generated a lot of goodwill in Madurai and reinforced its image as a cultural centre.

The charming story of the celestial wedding is re-enacted every year in Madurai. In April, the idols of Meenakshi and Shiva are wedded at the Meenakshi Temple with much pomp and grandeur. A procession carrying an idol of Vishnu simultaneously begins its march down the Azhagar Hills, making leisurely stops at various points along the way. The idol even gets a change of clothing at some of these stops! Finally, the deity reaches the River Vaigai. That's where he is politely informed that the wedding is already over. To this day, the idol has never crossed the river. And Madurai celebrates this wedding drama, year after year, with great pomp and ceremony.

Many couples renew their wedding vows along with Shiva and Meenakshi. Tens of thousands of people come from neighbouring villages to cheer on, as the newly

At the Azhagar Temple, Lord Vishnu goes by the name of Kallazhagar, a name which has been interpreted differently by different scholars. In Tamil, 'Azhagar' means 'the handsome one'. The deity used for the procession is also called Sundara Rajan, which means 'the handsome king'. But why Kallazhagar? One version says that this deity was worshipped by the Kalla community, a prominent ethnic group of farmers and soldiers who lived in this area. The handsome deity of the Kallas had to be Kallazhagar. Another version is that the word 'kalla' means thief in Tamil. Vishnu, in his handsome form stole everyone's heart, and so it is said that he is known as Kallazhagar. Nammalvar, the eighth century poet, calls him 'the mischievous thief who stole his heart'. The Azhagar Temple is considered a 'Divya Desam' meaning that it is one of the 108 most sacred shrines of Vishnu.

The procession of Lord Vishnu.

wed god and goddess are taken, aboard gigantic chariots, in a procession along the streets around the temple. These colourful, decked chariots are pulled by hand by the thousands of people who throng the streets on that day. The last day of this festival, when Vishnu reaches the river, is a public holiday in Madurai even today. The city watches in breathless anticipation, as Vishnu, piqued by the insult, returns in a huff to his hilltop temple.

Madurai has been witness to this family feud for over 400 years.

Chithirai festival

16

The Triumphs and Tragedies of Shah Jahan

TAJ MAHAL, AGRA

Perfect in its symmetry, a memorial in white –
This monument of love was a testament to a king's might;
He sat on the throne of the richest kingdom in the world,
But despite the power and riches, a tragic life unfurled;
The magnificent Taj Mahal, behind its beautiful facade,
Hides bloodcurdling tales of a system that was flawed.

The Taj Mahal has stood in Agra for over 350 years, telling, in its own muted way, the story of the Mughal emperor Shah Jahan. Between 1628 and 1658 CE, Shah Jahan ruled over the largest empire in India at the time. It was also the richest in the world, contributing nearly 25 per cent of the world's GDP.[1] In that rich, protected environment, arts and crafts flourished like never before. And the Taj Mahal is considered the pinnacle of Mughal architecture.

It is common knowledge that the Taj Mahal was built by a grief-stricken Shah Jahan as a monument to his

[1] GDP or Gross Domestic Product is the total value of all goods and services produced in a country in a year. This is a good measure of how rich a country is.

Mughal is the Persian word for Mongol and the Mughals trace their roots to Mongolia. This dynasty was established by Babur, a Turkic Mongol warrior who came from modern-day Uzbekistan. On his father's side, he was a descendant of Timur Lang, the most powerful ruler in the Islamic world at one time. On his mother's side, he was a descendant of the dreaded Mongol king, Genghis Khan, who founded one of the largest empires in world history. And Babur himself went on to establish a new dynasty in India.

beloved wife, Mumtaz Mahal. Shah Jahan demanded and ensured the best materials for the Taj; marble from Makrana in north-west India, turquoise from Tibet,

The Taj Mahal is a UNESCO World Heritage Site and one of the New Seven Wonders of the World. Taj Mahal literally means 'Crown Palace'. The Mughal chronicles call it the 'Rauzza-i-Munawwara' meaning 'the illustrious tomb'. The main structure came up between 1631 and 1643, but work continued until 1653. Over 22,000 workers and 1,000 elephants were employed in its construction. Shah Jahan spared no expense and sourced the finest material from all over the world. About 28 different types of gems were inlaid into the marble in beautiful patterns using a technique called *parchin kari* or 'pietra dura'. Every year, more than seven million tourists visit the Taj. Did you know that Taj Mahal, at 73 m, is actually taller than the Qutb Minar, the tallest brick minaret in the world?

The Taj Mahal

diamonds from the Deccan region in south India, jade from China and lapis lazuli from Afghanistan.

It makes you picture Shah Jahan as a man who could dream up graceful buildings, a man with an artistic eye and a sensitive soul.

Dig deeper, and behind the beautiful facade of the Taj lie blood-curdling stories: of cruel blindings, treacherous back-stabbing and brutal murders. While the Mughal emperors, seated on their exquisite thrones, seemed unshakeable in their strength, the entire royal family

Shah Jahan

was riven with jealousy and power struggles. Brothers viewed each other with suspicion, while uncles and nephews conspired behind closed doors. Sons connived to wrest the throne from their fathers, even while they were alive and well!

Take the case of Shah Jahan. He had four sons. His third son, Aurangzeb, was by far the most competent. But Shah Jahan showered much love on the firstborn, Dara Shikoh, and openly favoured him to succeed to the throne. Aurangzeb deeply resented this. That resentment festered until 1658, when Shah Jahan fell ill. An ugly war of succession instantly broke out among the siblings. Aurangzeb defeated Dara, humiliated him by parading him through the streets of Delhi, and then had him beheaded. He imprisoned his father, Shah Jahan, and crowned himself king. Aurangzeb went on to dispose of his other brothers as well. He executed one of his brothers on doubtful charges, and made another flee India for life. Shah Jahan spent his last years under house arrest in Agra. When he died, Aurangzeb even denied him a state funeral, and buried him without ceremony at the Taj Mahal.

Later, when his children grew up, Aurangzeb exiled one of his own sons and imprisoned two others. One of them went on to become the next king, but only after killing two of his siblings.

Was Aurangzeb an aberration, an outlier among the great Mughals? Not really. Shah Jahan himself had been a seasoned hand at this ruthless game of thrones. Let's look at how he came to power.

Shah Jahan was born to Emperor Jahangir, but was neither the eldest son, nor the favourite one. That position was occupied by Prince Khusrau, who was being groomed for the throne. Khusrau was the ideal heir to the throne – handsome, brave and very popular with the people. It was expected that he would inherit the throne, even edging his own father, Jahangir, out of the race. Jahangir didn't appreciate this at all and had no qualms about placing his son under house arrest. Khusrau escaped and fled Delhi but was captured again. This time, he was blinded, making him ineligible to be a ruler ever.

Shah Jahan now became the heir apparent. But Khusrau was still alive, and a potential threat. One night, assailants broke into his chamber and killed him. It is widely believed this was done on Shah Jahan's orders.

A few years later, in 1627, Jahangir died. At that time, Shah Jahan was campaigning in the Deccan, far away from the capital. Immediately, his stepbrother Shahryar proclaimed himself emperor. Shah Jahan rushed to Delhi, defeated Shahryar, and had him executed. As if that was not enough, a series of merciless executions followed: stepbrothers, cousins and all other potential rivals to the throne were done away with.

Was Shah Jahan overly cruel? Perhaps he was. But oddly enough, he was merely following the norms of the time. Had he not killed his competitors, they would

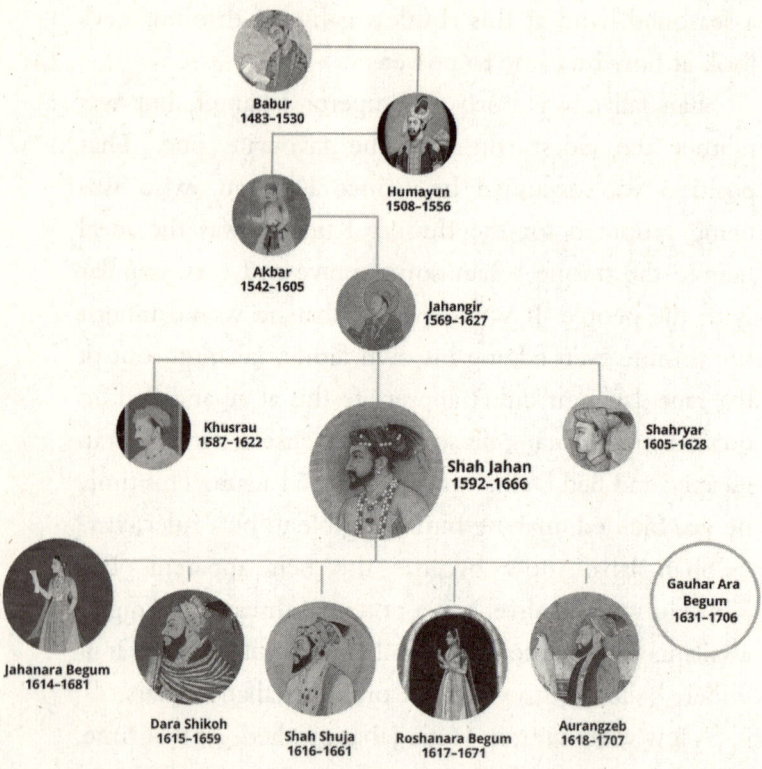

The Mughal family tree (an abridged version): from Babur to Aurangzeb

have killed him! But why was this family so violent? Were all these men heartless by nature?

Their actions might suggest that, but there was a deeper problem – the Mughal system of succession.

In most kingdoms, the eldest prince became the next king. This is called primogeniture. The Mughals, though, did it differently. Initially they tried to follow the system of their ancestors, the Mongols. It was called the coparcenary system, where the kingdom was divided between the sons. But soon, it turned into a mad, winner-takes-all scramble. Brothers, cousins and nephews raised armies and battled one another, until one prince was left standing. That survivor, the next king, was the toughest, and arguably the most suited to run the kingdom.

This succession system was violent, but it worked well for the Mughals, at least in the beginning. It was this system that made Shah Jahan the most triumphant of all Mughal kings. Ironically, he was also its most tragic victim.

The Mughal succession system had some unexpected fallouts. The vicious battles for the throne meant that there were very few eligible bachelors left alive. So, many Mughal princesses were forced to remain unmarried because they could not find grooms of equal status outside the Mughal clan. All three daughters of Shah Jahan never married. The system continued to play itself out, with weaker and weaker kings on the throne.

The succession system was clearly not working for the Mughals. Moreover, the repeated civil wars caused by family members fighting each other weakened the Mughal dynasty's control over the empire. In 1857, the last Mughal king, Bahadur Shah Zafar II, was deposed by the British.

These succession battles were not unique to the Mughals. Even Emperor Ashoka, the king who later helped spread Buddhism, came to power only after killing the crown prince and many of his stepbrothers. Centuries later, in the Vijayanagara Empire, the mighty

Krishnadevaraya's son-in-law placed the legal heirs under house arrest to take over the throne for himself. But while these kings were simply exceptions to the rule, for the Mughals, this was the norm.

Was one system better than the other? In primogeniture, the crown always went to the eldest son. The transition was predictable and smooth, and it did not fragment the kingdom. But there was no saying if the eldest son would turn out to be competent.

The Mughal system on the other hand, weeded out the 'weaklings', but succession was always fraught with uncertainty. It sat the most aggressive man on the throne. It put family members at loggerheads, resulting in much tragedy. The public execution of Dara Shikoh by his brother, Aurangzeb, was perhaps the starkest example of how ugly this system could get. And yet, in later years, Aurangzeb's daughter, Zubdat-un-Nissa, married

When Babur established the Mughal dynasty, he decided to follow a Central Asian tradition of dividing property between sons. His eldest son, Humayun, got the Indian territories, while another son, Kamran Mirza, got the Afghan territories; and there were a few other brothers who got nothing. When Babur died, all his sons who had been denied a part of his kingdom, revolted against Humayun – the eldest son and holder of the Indian territories. Kamran, who got the Afghan lands, wanted the Indian lands too. And so began the battles for succession in the Mughal dynasty.

Dara Shikoh's son, Sipihr Shikoh; and Aurangzeb's son, Mohammad Azam, married Dara Shikoh's daughter, Jani Begum. Clearly, the enmity between Mughal siblings was not a matter of vengeance, but a means of survival.

Shah Jahan lived by an unforgiving system that put him on the throne of the richest kingdom in the world. But that very same system extracted a hefty price in return. Shah Jahan was indeed a triumphant king; and yet, he was a man who lived a terribly tragic life.

17

The French Generals Who Lost to Their Own Side

RAJ NIVAS, PONDICHERRY

The French generals in India faced
An impossible adversary that kept them on their toes –
Not Indian kings, nor the British in India,
Oh, the French themselves were their biggest foes!
One French General defeated the British in India,
Battling them hard on land and in water,
But his indecisive king back in France
Handed the territories back to the British on a platter!
Then came another brave general
Who gave his all to hold fort
But ended up in a prison in France,
And was then beheaded on the orders of a French court!

The Raj Nivas is the official residence of the lieutenant governor of Pondicherry (now called Puducherry). Not too long ago, this building was called 'Le Palais du Gouverneur', the 'palace of the governor' - the French governor. For nearly 300 years, Pondicherry was the headquarters of French India.

The British East India Company, a small trading institution from England, was set up in 1600 to trade

Raj Nivas

in India. Their first ships landed in India in 1608. At that time colonizing India was furthest from the minds. But soon, they established their stronghold in Madras, modern-day Chennai. Their biggest rivals in Europe, the French, followed soon after. The French East India Company was set up in 1664 and their first ships landed in India in 1674. They settled down in Pondicherry, not far from Chennai, and made it their centre for trade.

Over the next 300 years, the British went on to control a large part of the Indian subcontinent. The French, however, controlled only a few small territories across the country.

Why did the French get left behind? History books offer many explanations. But the biggest reason was that the French were fighting a difficult battle against an impossible adversary – the French themselves!

Both the British and the French East India Companies were set up to trade with India. While the objectives were similar, they were fundamentally very different. The British East India Company was a private monopolistic company. The French East India Company, on the other hand, was controlled by the French government. This meant that the British generals could take decisions on the spot, while the French had to take approvals from the king of France. That was not ideal, because their ruler, in the mid-1700s, was Louis XV – not the most decisive of kings. And he wasn't at all sure what he wanted to do with his Indian colonies.

As a result, the French officials in India were never sure why they were in India. Was it to build trade, or an empire? Lacking leadership, they were often forced to take matters into their own hands. And then, they blamed each other for the disastrous results.

In 1742, a clever and ambitious man named Joseph Francois Dupleix became Governor General of French India. The present-day Raj Nivas in Pondicherry was commissioned during his time. His dream was to defeat the British, make India a French colony and rule over

---

Pondicherry has a beautiful coastline. Before Indian independence, the Marine Drive was dotted with buildings of the French colonial style of architecture. This was the 'White Town' of Pondicherry where the French lived. The most important building on the shoreline was the Governor's mansion. The building was commissioned during the rule of the French governor Francois Dupleix, and called 'Le Palais du Gouverneur', meaning 'the Governor's Palace'. In 1761, the British defeated the French and occupied Pondicherry, and this building fell into disrepair. Then in 1766, when the French got the city back, the building was remodelled and renovated. Today, it is called Raj Nivas and is the official residence of the lieutenant governor of Pondicherry. Experts classify the architecture as the Rococo style, which became popular in France in the 1700s.

it. The British, obviously, did not like the idea one bit. In 1746, they began a naval blockade of Pondicherry. Dupleix immediately sent an SOS to the governor of nearby Mauritius, naval commander Bertrand Francois Mahé, Comte de La Bourdonnais, a brilliant naval commander who knew the Indian Ocean like the back of his hand. Mauritius was also a French colony, but Dupleix outranked La Bourdonnais. He immediately sailed to Pondicherry with a small fleet and easily broke the blockade. Dupleix was relieved, but not content. He ordered La Bourdonnais to attack Madras, a thriving British colony. La Bourdonnais protested that he had not come prepared for a prolonged battle, but Dupleix overruled him.

La Bourdonnais's navy bombarded Madras so heavily that the British surrendered. The victorious La Bourdonnais imposed a crippling fine on the British

Emblems of the British East India Company (*left*) and the French East India Company (*right*)

colony, but Dupleix was not happy. He wanted La Bourdonnais to drive the British out completely. He raved and ranted at La Bourdonnais, and the frustrated commander returned to Mauritius in a huff.

To his horror, he found that Dupleix had engineered corruption charges against him and replaced him with a new governor. He decided to complain to the bosses in France. But when La Bourdonnais reached Paris, he was thrown into the Bastille prison without a trial. He was eventually acquitted in 1751. But by then, he had lost his wealth, health and dignity. He died, a broken man, in 1754.

What happened to Dupleix? Just three years after the hard-earned victory in Madras, the French government in Paris signed a treaty with the British, simply returning Madras to them in exchange for other concessions. An unhappy Dupleix decided to take matters into his own hands. Unfortunately for him, he completely misread the political mood in Paris.

Dupleix grew up during the rule of Louis XIV when France was a superpower with ambitions to expand their might. But after him, the political climate in France had changed. The new ruler, Louis XV, was a fickle leader with no clear vision for France, leave alone a clear mandate for the French East India Company. But Dupleix ploughed on with his plans to colonize India. He built up a large army and manipulated local kings. All this cost money and Dupleix demanded more funds from Paris. They refused, and ordered Dupleix to stop squandering money. By now, Dupleix was in too deep. He started using his own personal wealth for the campaigns, assuming that Paris would soon see things his way. But they did not. In 1754, they dismissed Dupleix and forced him to return home.

Dupleix pleaded with his bosses to reimburse the vast personal fortune that he had spent in India. His pleas were ignored. And Joseph Francois Dupleix, the man who could have turned India into a grand French colony, died in relative poverty in 1763.

Ironically, just a couple of years after Dupleix was dismissed, King Louis XV flip-flopped again, and decided to do exactly what Dupleix had intended – set up a strong French colony in India. He chose a man named General Thomas Arthur, Comte de Lally for the job. Lally was known to be brave and loyal, but also sharp-tongued and brutally blunt. And that earned him many enemies. Lally was appointed the Governor General of French India. What followed was a series of misfortunes for him.

Just as Lally was about to set sail for India, he got the news that King Louis XV had suddenly cut his budget by a third, and diverted a part of his army to Canada. Lally was too proud to demand his dues, so he took what was offered and set sail.

When he reached Pondicherry, he was welcomed with a 21-gun naval salute. And it was just his luck that they misfired and blew a hole right through his ship. Nobody died, but it was an ominous beginning to his tenure in India.

In Pondicherry, Lally discovered that the French officers were notoriously inefficient. His heavy-handed way of straightening them out only made them more uncooperative. Lally couldn't care less. He had a war to win. He went ahead with his plans to attack the British. His army quickly besieged Madras. Vice Admiral Comte d'Ache, who had been officially deputed to assist Lally, provided the naval support.

Anne Antoine, Comte d'Aché was an easy-going man who did not share Lally's passionate commitment to French interests in India. He began well, and effectively blockaded the Madras port. But then, he changed his mind. Bang in the middle of the naval battle, the admiral decided that his ships needed repair, and sailed away to Mauritius. Although d'Ache had left behind a smaller contingent of naval soldiers with Lally, the French navy had practically deserted the French army!

Not one to give up, Lally decided to engage with the British on land. That's when the native soldiers of the Pondicherry army mutinied. They had not received their salaries, because the French king had cut the budgets. Somehow Lally rallied them on and fought a last-ditch battle at a place called Wandiwash, today called Vandavasi. Midway through the battle, the contingent of naval soldiers left behind by d'Ache simply deserted him and fled! Lally was forced to retreat to Pondicherry. The British immediately besieged Pondicherry and cut off all routes of escape. Lally held on, for one whole year, waiting for assistance to come from France. The French king remained indecisive, and no help came.

In a final desperate bid, Lally sent a small contingent to quietly creep around the British soldiers and surprise them from behind. As luck would have it, the French soldiers miscalculated the distance and popped up right in front of the British! By now, the besieged French in Pondicherry were on the brink of starvation. A dispirited Lally surrendered in 1761.

The French government was thoroughly embarrassed. They needed a scapegoat, and they found an easy one in Lally. They announced that Lally had secretly sided with the British and that it was his treachery that had caused the French to lose. Lally was horrified. But, by then, he was a prisoner in England. He begged his captors to let him go to France to defend his honour. The British, very sportingly, did just that.

As soon as Lally reached Paris, he was arrested and thrown into the Bastille prison, without so much as a trial. After all, the government couldn't afford for the truth to come out. A rigged trial took place two years later. Lally defended himself in the only way he knew – he abused the judges! Lally was found guilty of treason. He was to be beheaded. But Lally's misfortunes continued to dog him. The first blow of the sword only split his skull and it took a second, more violent blow to end his suffering. This brave general, who had faced many powerful enemies, was ultimately defeated by his own people. In later

During his lifetime, Lally had made many enemies. That included many honourable men, who could have helped him but for his foul temper. And yet, when Lally's case was reopened, help came from unexpected sources. One of them was the famous French activist and philosopher Voltaire, who despised him for his abusive tongue. However, he knew that Lally was a principled man, who could never commit treason. When King Louis XVI succeeded Louis XV, Voltaire wrote to him, appealing to reopen the case.

An even more surprising was support from Sir Eyre Coote, the English general who had routed and imprisoned Lally in Pondicherry. He praised Lally with these generous words: "Nobody had a higher idea than I of General Lally, who to my knowledge has struggled against obstacles, which I believed unconquerable, and has conquered them; nobody at the same time, is more his enemy than I, seeing him achieve those triumphs at the prejudice of my nation. There is certainly not a second man in all India who could have managed to keep on foot, for so long a period, an army without pay, and without any kind of assistance." This strengthened Lally's case further.

years, his son had the case reopened again in court. Surprisingly, the strongest support came from Sir Eyre Coote, the same British General who had defeated and captured Lally in Pondicherry!

The French flipped sides again and, finally, Lally's name was cleared by the new king, Louis XVI.

In the following decades, the French and the British fought many battles in India. But more often than not, the French had to retreat with a bloody nose. In most cases, it was the French government that shot itself in the foot, by failing those who could have won victories for them.

And yet, despite these many fiascos, the French outlasted the British in India. In 1947, when India got its independence from the British, the new Indian government was certain that the French would leave too. But they held on. Finally, on 1 November 1954, after enormous pressure from the Indian government, they agreed to cede Pondicherry to India. They only needed a formal ratification from their parliament. That formality took another eight years. On 16 August 1962, the French finally packed up and left. So Pondicherry celebrates three independence days – 15 August (Indian Independence Day), 16 August (Transfer of Power Day) and 1 November (Pondicherry Liberation Day).

18

The Journey of a 2,000-year-old Bead

KEELADI

Deep underground, on potsherds were found
Graffiti similar to the marks on the Mohenjo-daro mound;
The exciting new discoveries in Keeladi show
Glimpses of an advanced civilization from 2,600 years ago!

In 2015, in a little village on the banks of the River Vaigai, near Madurai in Tamil Nadu, archaeologists unearthed ancient artefacts dating back to the sixth century BCE. These included potsherds with inscriptions in an ancient script called the Tamil–Brahmi script. As they dug deeper, they found more potsherds but with marks in a different script – one that looked remarkably similar to the script found in the Indus Valley Civilization in north-western India from a good 4,500 years ago. That script still remains undeciphered. What could be the link between these two civilizations that were separated by at least 1,000 years and over 3,000 km?

This discovery created a flutter among scholars. It seemed to offer an important missing piece in the puzzle of the evolution of Indian civilization. Why was this discovery so important? To answer that, let's first look at what we know about ancient Indian civilizations this far.

The oldest Indian civilization that we know of is the Indus Valley Civilization, which goes back to at least 2600 BCE. It spanned a long stretch of present-day north-western India, Pakistan and Afghanistan, and it was one of the largest civilizations in the world. Sometime around 1600 BCE, the Indus Valley Civilization faded away. We still don't know why. It was followed by the Vedic Age – another vast civilization that centred around the Gangetic plains of north India, lasting until about 500 BCE. It was during this time that India's Vedic literature was composed.

But what about south India? Weren't there ancient civilizations in south India too?

For a long time, people assumed that civilization in south India was no more than 2,300 years old, going back to the third century BCE. That's because there was no concrete evidence of any older settlement – no ruins of a city, for example, such as there were in the Indus Valley sites of Harappa, Mohenjo-daro and Lothal. But many archaeologists rejected that notion. Backing them up was an ancient corpus of Tamil writings, called the Sangam period literature. These poems, composed roughly between 300 BCE and 300 CE described a grand ancient Tamil civilization. Many archaeologists believed that if they searched hard enough, they would find physical evidence of that time. Keeladi seems to offer that evidence. Some of the artefacts unearthed there have been dated to 580 BCE. That pushes back the timeline of ancient Tamil civilization by nearly 300 years.

What specifically did they find at Keeladi? To begin with, they found many potsherds – broken pieces of pottery – buried in different layers underground. As time passes, old remains tend to slip deeper and deeper underground, so potsherds found in deeper layers are generally older than those found closer to the surface. Many of these potsherds carry inscriptions on them. Those in the uppermost layers are inscribed in an early Tamil script called 'Tamili', also called 'Tamil-Brahmi'. The middle layers have some Tamili inscriptions along with other scratch marks that are called 'graffiti' marks. Graffito in Italian literally means 'a scratch'. And the deepest layers have only the graffiti marks on them. And it is these graffiti marks that bear an uncanny resemblance to the graffiti found in the Indus Valley excavations nearly 3,000 km away!

Why is this significant? Because it tells us the story of how scripts may have evolved in India.

The oldest readable Indian script that we know of is called Brahmi. All Indian scripts are said to have evolved from this mother script, which was in use around the third century BCE. At that time, the languages spoken in north India were Prakrit and Sanskrit, while the language in the south was Tamil. All these languages were written in the Brahmi script. Over many centuries, the Brahmi script evolved into the Nagari script in the north. Down south, it evolved into a script called Tamili or Tamil-

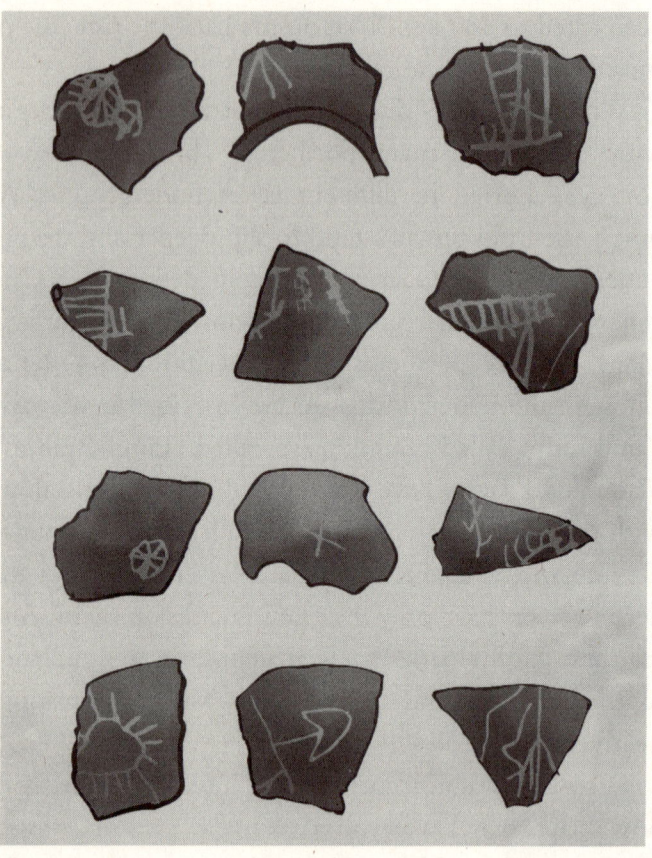

Potsherds with graffiti

Not everyone agrees with this theory. There is another school of thought that suggests that the Tamili script predates Brahmi, and evolved from an ancient script called Proto-Tamil. At present, there is not enough evidence to prove or disprove either of these theories.

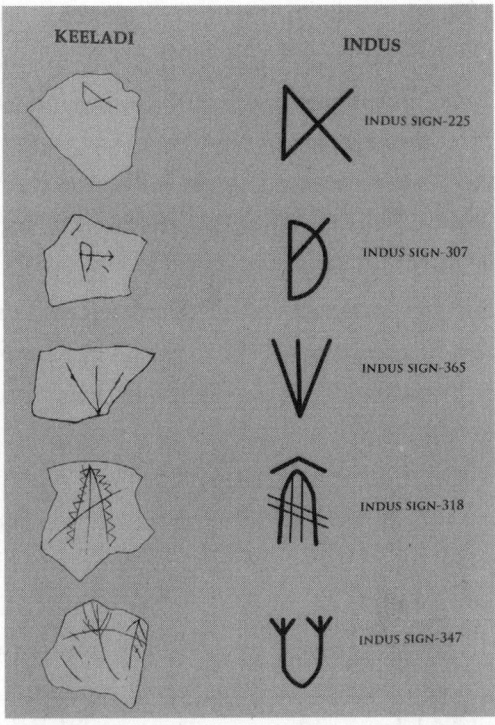

KEELADI	INDUS
	INDUS SIGN-225
	INDUS SIGN-307
	INDUS SIGN-365
	INDUS SIGN-318
	INDUS SIGN-347

Comparison of Keeladi and Indus Valley Civilization graffiti

Brahmi, which eventually evolved into the modern-day Tamil script.

Some archaeologists now believe that Brahmi itself may have evolved from the graffiti marks found in the Indus Valley and at the Keeladi excavations. Does that mean that the people of the Indus Valley came to south India and settled there? Some historians think so. But then, there are others who suggest that this find implies the exact opposite – that there were thriving settlements in south India much before that time; an ancient Tamil civilization that interacted with and influenced the language and cultures of north Indian civilizations. The story is still unfolding, and we don't have all the answers yet.

Do we know what kind of place Keeladi was? A clue comes from a little orange bead that was found at the excavation site.

Sangam literature tells us that the ancient Tamils had a flourishing trade in gems. The orange bead was one of the many excavated from Keeladi, and it has a figure of a boar carved on its surface. It is a carnelian intaglio (or engraved) bead. Today carnelian is not very expensive, but it was one of the many semi-precious stones from India that were in high demand in those days. These gemstones were mined in the river basins of south India.

It is likely that this little carnelian also originated there. It would have to be shaped and polished, and for that, it would have either travelled south-east towards the ancient bead-making centre of Arikamedu, near modern-day Puducherry, or north-west towards the stonework centre of Khambhat in Gujarat, a region that has evidence of bead and stone work going back thousands of years. Once it was crafted into a perfect shape, the bead would have gone to the ancient port city of Muziris, near Kochi in Kerala. Muziris was a busy port, one where many Roman ships came to trade. The Romans loved precious stones, and their master jewellers were famous for their skill in cutting complex designs into stone, just like the boar on the orange bead.

Once carved, the little bead returned to Muziris, and eventually ended up at Keeladi. Archaeologists believe that Keeladi may have been a market from where people bought and sold beads.

Isn't it amazing how much a tiny bead can tell us? Among other things, it tells us that Keeladi was more connected with the rest of India and the world 2,600 years ago than it is today.

What was life like at Keeladi? Archaeologists found small pieces of tiles that were used to play hopscotch, a game that is still played world over. They also found dice and many terracotta gamesmen. Sangam literature mentions a game called '*dhaayakattam*', somewhat similar to Ludo, which is popular even today. Other artefacts found at Keeladi include specialized tools that tell us that the people of Keeladi could spin their own yarn and therefore, manufacture cloth. They also found ivory combs, bangles and gold ornaments here. All this tells us that this society must have been stable, perhaps even affluent.

The buildings in Keeladi seem to be neatly positioned, and every brick is of the same standard specification (something that stands out in the Indus Valley cities too). Terracotta pipes and ring wells have been found, indicating that the residents knew how to channel in fresh water and dispose of dirty water more than 2,600 years ago. These are signs of urbanization, and hence archaeologists believe Keeladi may have been an urban settlement.

Ring well

Despite all these finds, archaeologists are hesitant to call Keeladi a residential site. Usually, inhabited sites yield a lot of human bones. At Keeladi, there were none to be found, and that puzzled archaeologists. But as they expanded the area under excavation, they reached a village called Kondagai, not far from Keeladi. And there, they unearthed many well-preserved skeletons.

Is Keeladi the oldest evidence of human habitation in south India? While Keeladi has certainly pushed back the accepted timeline of ancient Tamil civilization, it is neither the first find nor the oldest of such sites in Tamil Nadu. Adichanallur, a site near Korkai in southern Tamil Nadu has been under archaeological scrutiny since 1876! In 2004, an archaeologist named Dr Satyamurthy had the remains found at Adichanallur carbon dated. The results showed them to be from 905–696 BCE! Close to Keeladi is another village called Agaram, where archaeologists have unearthed microlithic tools, which are small stones sharpened to be used as tools. Archaeologists believe these tools may be from the Neolithic period, which was roughly between 8000 and 3000 BCE. Remember, Keeladi is dated to just about 580 BCE. This suggests that people have been living in these parts for a very, very long time! Did you know that the oldest stone age site in India is also in Tamil Nadu? In 1863, at a site in Pallavaram, very close to Chennai, a young British geologist named Robert Bruce Foote found a hand axe used by Palaeolithic people. And this tool is believed to be at least 200,000 years old!

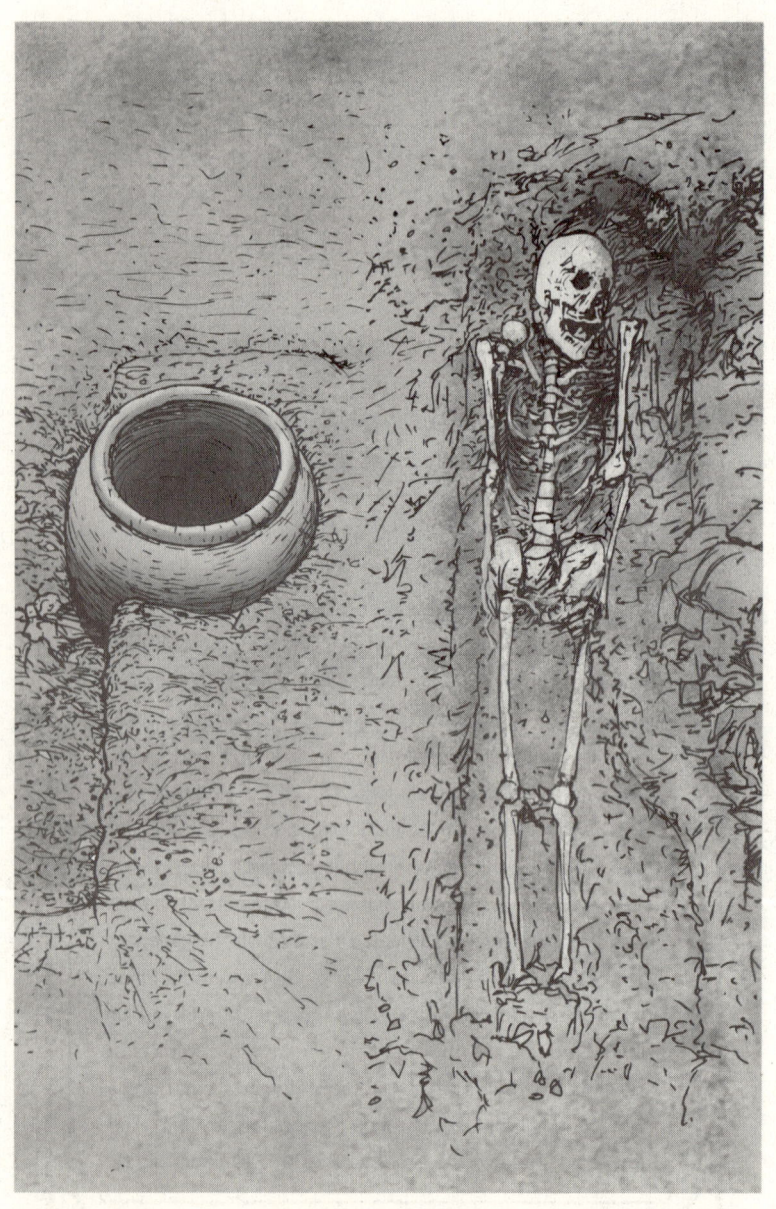

Burial urn and skeleton

Archaeologists take a ghoulish delight in graves, because the artefacts buried with the dead body tell them a lot about the people of those times. In Kondagai, along with the skeletons, archaeologists found over 40 burial urns. These earthen jars stored the ashes of the dead who were commonly cremated. And sometimes, tools and weapons of the dead person were also placed in the urn, along with some food. Many such ancient burial urns have been found across Tamil Nadu. Recently, a grain of rice found at Korkai, a settlement along the River Thamirabarani, also called the River Porunai in southern Tamil Nadu, was scientifically dated to 1155 BCE! And that tells us that civilization in south India is much older than we believed it to be until recently.

The Keeladi excavations have certainly given a fresh perspective to what was going on in ancient south India. But the most exciting part of this story is that only a tenth of the identified area has been excavated so far. And it is likely that further digs will bring us more answers, and perhaps throw up many more questions too.

19

The Rise and Fall of the Richest Man on Earth

FALAKNUMA PALACE, HYDERABAD

His garage housed over 150 cars, the finest of the fine,
Why ever not, 'cause he happened to own the world's only
diamond mine!
His gems and jewels were stashed away in all nooks
and pockets,
His fabulous collection of emeralds just kept spilling out of
brown paper packets!
So rich he was that he used an incredibly expensive diamond
as a paperweight;
He was the richest man in the world, the ruler of
Hyderabad state.

In 1937, *Time* magazine published a photograph of a little-known man on its cover. It dubbed him as the richest man in the world then. The picture was of Mir Osman Ali Khan, the Nizam or ruler of an Indian princely state called Hyderabad. With that, this king, who ruled Hyderabad between 1911 and 1948, had suddenly walked into the spotlight.

But just how much wealth did one need to qualify for the coveted title of the world's richest man? Many estimates have been made. *Time*'s own calculation was that the Nizam was worth about USD 2 billion. Of course, that included a fabulous collection of gems and jewels too. The *Daily Mail*, a UK newspaper, once estimated that his pearl collection was large enough to pave the entire Piccadilly Square, a massive square right in the middle of London. Visitors wrote about how he casually stored the pearls in ordinary sacks and occasionally got his servants to air them out —a task that took them three full days! *Forbes* magazine would later declare him one of the five richest men in history. According to *Forbes*'s calculations, the present–day value of the Nizam's assets was over USD 210 billion! He owned about 150 cars, of which 50 were Rolls Royces, the most expensive luxury cars in the world then! In the time he ruled, his entire fleet of Rolls Royces had only travelled less than 2,000 km. He just had too many cars!

Of the many palaces he owned one was the historic Falaknuma Palace. Literally 'the mirror of the sky', this milky white palace in Hyderabad is today an ultra luxury hotel. Its massive ballrooms and plush bedrooms, a dining hall that could seat over 100 guests, lit by glittering Venetian chandeliers, and verdant and spacious gardens were all witness to the extravagant lifestyle of the Nizams. For all its opulence, the Nizam didn't even live here; he merely used this as a guest house.

So how did one man get to become so unbelievably wealthy? The answer is easy. He simply inherited a kingdom that was rich and relatively peaceful. It all

Falaknuma Palace was built by Sir Viqar-ul-Umra, who was the prime minister and brother-in-law of Mir Mahbub Ali Khan, the sixth Nizam of Hyderabad. It was designed by William Mard Marret, a brilliant English architect, constructed with the finest materials, and furnished and decorated with the priciest fittings from all over the world. It took 10 years to complete, and in 1893, it was one of the finest palaces in the world. The problem was that it cost over four million rupees, a monstrous amount in those days. Sir Viqar was on the verge of bankruptcy, but there was no one who could buy it from him. In the meantime, he had invited the then Nizam, Mahbub Ali, to stay with him in the palace. The Nizam did stay with him for a few days, and then, he became the owner of the spanking new royal residence! One story says that the Nizam loved the palace, so Sir Viqar offered it to him as a gift. The Nizam gracefully accepted it, but immediately paid the full cost to Sir Viqar. Osman Ali Khan inherited the palace, which was passed on to his grandson Mukarram Jah, when Hyderabad became part of India. However, he had no resources to maintain the palace, so it was converted into a high-end hotel.

began in 1657 when a Turkoman noble from Central Asia named Abid Khan decided to throw in his lot with Mughal emperor Aurangzeb, who at that time was still a prince and the governor of the Deccan. Abid Khan stood by Aurangzeb through a gory war of succession. In 1658, when Aurangzeb became the Mughal emperor, Abid Khan's family became very influential in the

Falaknuma Palace

Mughal court. In 1713, his grandson, Qamaruddin, was appointed as Nizam, meaning 'governor' in Urdu, of the Mughal territory known as Hyderabad–Deccan. He was the first Nizam and the founder of the 'Asaf Jahi' dynasty. From then on, all his descendants took the title 'Nizam' and continued to rule till 1948.

After Aurangzeb's death, the Mughal Empire started disintegrating. The Nizams held their territory together, largely remaining neutral, warding off invaders and forming friendly alliances. They allied with the French and later with the British who were trying to establish their political power in India. Yet, practically for nearly 250 years, they ran the kingdom with complete autonomy.

In those days Hyderabad was a large kingdom, nearly the size of present-day UK. It consisted of today's

Telangana, and included parts of present-day Andhra Pradesh, Karnataka, Maharashtra and Chhattisgarh. The land was fertile, and the feudal lords collected large rents and filled the Nizam's treasury. More significantly, the world's only diamond mine, Golconda, was in the kingdom of the Nizams. Until the 1900s it was the only functional diamond mine in the whole world. It produced many famous diamonds including the Koh-i-noor and the Hope diamond.

In 1911, Osman Ali Khan, the seventh Nizam, inherited all this glorious wealth. By then, the British were ruling over most of the Indian subcontinent. Osman Ali Khan very astutely allied with the British and lavished gifts on them. During the World Wars he financed battleships and two Spitfire squadrons for the British. In return, the British bestowed fancy titles on him. While all other Indian kings were addressed as 'your highness', the British addressed him as 'your exalted highness'.

However, perhaps because he had so much wealth, Osman Ali had a bizarre relationship with money. For instance, he stored his humongous collection of emeralds in brown-paper packets. The Jacob diamond, an enormous South African diamond, which his father had bought, was casually placed in an old sock and forgotten. Years later, Osman Ali discovered it and put it to a marginally better use. He used this incredibly expensive diamond as a paperweight!

There are stories, some perhaps apocryphal, of how miserly he was. Despite the bizarre rumours, he was

Mir Osman Ali Khan

responsible for many developments in Hyderabad. He introduced electricity and irrigation, built hospitals and reservoirs, and set up the famous Osmania University to further the study of the arts and sciences. He readily gave away 14,000 acres of land to be distributed to the landless. For all this, he is called the 'architect of modern Hyderabad'.

Change, however, was just around the corner. By the 1940s, the British had decided to leave India, partitioning the subcontinent into independent India and Pakistan. Most rulers of princely states signed treaties with either India or Pakistan, merging their kingdoms with either of the two new nations.

The Nizam, however, had different ideas. He fondly hoped to run an independent state in the middle of India just as his ancestors had done in the past. He desperately tried to muster international support for his idea. The British, already battered by the World Wars, ignored his feelers. He went to the United Nations, but got only a lukewarm reception from there. And newborn India was snapping at his heels, insisting he join with it. Things came to a head when a local militant group caught on to the idea of an independent Hyderabad, threatening peace in the area. The Indian government acted quickly, and sent in its army. In a 'police action' lasting just four days, the Indian army took complete control of the state. Left with no choice, Osman Ali Khan finally merged Hyderabad with India. The Indian government appointed him as the governor to manage the transition till 1956. After that, he led a quiet life until his death in 1967.

And whatever happened to all the pearls and gemstones? Once Hyderabad merged with India, the new Indian government considered them to be a national treasure. Not wanting them to leave the country, the Indian government bought a large portion of the Nizam's personal jewel collection at an agreed price of Rs 2.2 billion. Today, the Nizam's huge collection of jewels, including the famous Jacob's diamond, lies in the vaults of the Reserve Bank of India, Mumbai. Once in a while, they are displayed for the public viewing, reminding them of the Nizam's glittering past.

Another huge assortment of treasures is displayed at the Nizam's Museum in the Purani Haveli, the old palace of the Nizam dynasty in Hyderabad. This collection includes gifts that the Nizam received from well-wishers and from anyone who came to meet him, as was the tradition in those days. These include gold and silver models of major buildings, silver coffee cups studded with diamonds, golden boxes studded with gems...the list goes on. One can also see a small portion of the massive car collection that the Nizam once had – 1930 Rolls Royces, Jaguars, Packards and others. The richest man in the world certainly had a befitting lifestyle!

20

Robert Clive: The Man Who Laid the Foundation of the Raj

PALASHI MONUMENT, PALASHI

A misfit in his school, a teenage bully,
He came to town as a lowly clerk;
But he came into his own and transformed fully
When he took on a soldier's work.
A military genius, a greedy speculator,
and an imperialist to the core –
It is undisputed that no one else impacted
the fortunes of the British in India more

There is a nondescript little village called Palashi in the state of West Bengal. Amidst its jute and sugar-cane fields lie scattered some small shrines, memorials and obelisks. These structures, in and around Palashi, honour soldiers who lost their lives in the Battle of Plassey fought here in 1757. It was an encounter that changed the course of Indian history.

In the mid-1700s, the powerful Mughals, who ruled from Delhi, were weakening, resulting in political instability in the country. It was also the time the

THE PALASHI MONUMENT

Near the banks of River Bhagirathi and about 7 km from the Plassey Railway Station, lies the Palashi Monument. This is where the Battle of Plassey took place in 1757. Over the years, the river, when it changed course, has washed away parts of the original battlefield. What remains today is a bust of Siraj-ud-Daulah, a tall obelisk – called the Palashi Monument – commemorating the battle, and three smaller obelisks for three Bengal commanders who died leading the charge.

The monument commemorates the fallen soldiers and generals of Siraj-ud-Daulah's army. But, interestingly, this landmark battle itself was almost a non-event. The British lost fewer than 30 men in the day's action. In comparison, the Bengal army lost about 500 men, just a fraction of their 50,000 strong army. Higher casualties were known to have occurred in lesser battles. The entire battle was won by Clive's chicanery and Mir Jafar's treachery and not by valour. Next to the monument is a statue of Siraj-ud-Daulah. This too is ironic, because the Nawab fled the field without raising his sword.

The only brave act was by Mir Madan Khan, a loyal commander of Siraj-ud-Daulah's army. He unwittingly led a charge right into the British artillery and was knocked out. At a little distance from the Palashi Monument is an obscure memorial with three obelisks marking the spot where Mir Madan and two of his comrades fell. They were the real heroes of Plassey! Today this place is maintained by the Archaeological Survey of India.

Palashi Monument

European presence in India began to grow. The British and the French East India Companies, which had come to India in the previous century to trade, were now aggressively competing for dominance in India. Some Indian kings had permitted them to set up trading stations and, gradually, these companies began to fortify them.

The more dominant of these trading groups, the British had trading stations in erstwhile Bombay, Madras and Calcutta with a fort in each place. In 1756, the British decided to strengthen Fort William, their base in Calcutta. The ruler or nawab of Bengal, Siraj-ud-Daulah, did not approve of this and ordered them to stop, but the British simply ignored him. And so, the 23-year-old ruler attacked Fort William and defeated the British. Many of the captured British soldiers died in custody. The British were furious and immediately sent troops from Madras to fight Siraj-ud-Daulah.

This small army of 3,000 soldiers was commanded by an enterprising man named Robert Clive. He reached Calcutta and recaptured Fort William easily in a surprise pre-dawn strike. But the nawab had a bigger army and the challenge now was to fend off any retaliation from him. Clive shrewdly reached out to the nawab's army commander, Mir Jafar, and negotiated a devious deal. Clive offered to make Mir Jafar the ruler of Bengal if he supported the British. What followed was the Battle of Palashi (Plassey), where Mir Jafar and his troops treacherously stood by as mute spectators, while the British army quickly defeated the rest of Siraj-ud-Daulah's

THE BLACK HOLE INCIDENT

In June 1756, Siraj- ud-Daulah laid siege to Fort William in Calcutta. Only a small contingent (estimated at around 146) defended the fort, enabling the others to escape. This contingent surrendered on Siraj's promise that they would not be harmed.

Siraj gave orders to secure the prisoners and went to rest. After he left, the prisoners were stripped to the bare minimum clothing and thrown into a basement prison approximately 14 feet by 18 feet. The exact number stuffed into this small room is disputed. It is said that it was at least 64, but it could have been more. Accounts are not clear whether this was Siraj's order or a decision made by vengeful underlings in Siraj's army. Since it was the height of summer, the soldiers were dehydrated and overwhelmed by the heat. They tried to bribe the guards to open the door but were unsuccessful. In a frenzy, the men clambered over each other to reach the ventilator of the basement. The ensuing stampede killed some of them. By the next morning it is estimated that 43 of the prisoners had died due to asphyxiation (some chroniclers estimate a higher number). The original 'Black Hole' does not exist any more because Fort William was subsequently renovated. In 1901, a memorial obelisk for British soldiers who had died, was raised by Viceroy Curzon at Dalhousie Square (BBD Bagh), Calcutta. However, in subsequent years, freedom fighters objected to the monument and it was shifted to St John's Church, Calcutta, where it remains today.

The phrase 'Black Hole' has now entered common vocabulary, due to this incident. In the early 1960s, Princeton University astrophysicist Robert Dicke was moved enough by this event to name 'gravitationally collapsed objects where even light gets sucked in' as 'black holes'.

army. The nawab himself was later captured and killed by Mir Jafar's men.

With this victory, the British gained control of Bengal, one of the richest kingdoms in India at that time. They appointed Mir Jafar as a puppet ruler of Bengal. The East India Company now indirectly managed Bengal through Mir Jafar and made huge profits out of this conflict. Now it was no longer a mere trading company but one that controlled a large territory. Robert Clive also profited from the war. He got several personal gifts from Mir Jafar, including large tracts of land. When he returned to England in 1760, Clive was worth over GBP 45 million in today's value. He came to be known as 'Clive of India' for turning around British fortunes.

But then, this was not the first time that Clive had exhibited spunk and initiative. In 1751, King Wallajah of Arcot, a British ally, was in big trouble. His rival, Chanda Sahib, had occupied his capital, Arcot, chased him to Trichy (Tiruchirappalli) and besieged him there. To complicate matters, Chanda Sahib had the support of the French. While the British scrambled for ways to break the siege, Clive thought outside the box. Clive offered to lead an attack on Arcot with a small force, if he was made a captain at the end of it. Most of Chanda Sahib's army was in Trichy, leaving the capital, Arcot, vulnerable. He managed to capture Arcot with ease. Chanda Sahib's soldiers and French troops from Pondicherry rushed to Arcot. But Clive doggedly held the fort, leading risky charges, until British reinforcements came. In the

Robert Clive

British eyes, he was now a maverick commander who could not be defeated.

Clive's biographers have wondered if he always had this brazen streak? He did. As a child he was a bully and a complete nuisance to his teachers at school in London. He had to change schools often. As a teenager, he bullied local shopkeepers into paying protection money. In those days, such social misfits in England often found a new life in far-flung British colonies. In 1744, his father arranged a clerical job for him in the East India Company at Fort St George in Madras (now Chennai).

Clive tried hard to find his feet in a new environment, but he found life in the small city of Madras dull and tedious. Deeply frustrated, he attempted suicide, twice, and failed. However, he found relief in the Company library and spent hours reading.

In 1746, the French attacked Madras and took many people, including Clive, prisoner. But Clive used his wits to escape from prison and fled to Fort St David in Cuddalore, a British colony 175 km away. There he met Major Stringer Lawrence, the commander of the fort, who was at the time putting together a band of soldiers to fight the French. The Madras regiment that he created there is the oldest regiment of the Indian Army. He invited Clive to join that small brigade. And with that, Clive found his true calling as a military man, fighting many battles under Major Lawrence's guidance.

Although his career was doing well, Clive constantly struggled with mental and physical ailments. At the age of 27, he decided to retire to England. But once he got there, Clive found the quiet English life extremely dull. In 1755, he accepted another posting to India as Deputy Governor in command of Fort St David, Cuddalore. And it was from there that he went to fight the Battle of Plassey.

His victory in the Battle of Plassey so impressed the board of directors of the East India Company that they made him governor of Calcutta, twice. As governor, Clive focused on improving the efficiency of the workers of the Company. Ironically, many of his reforms were aimed at reducing corruption among British officers. And this made Clive rather unpopular among the British in India.

His enemies waited to strike back. In 1773, a parliamentary committee investigated him for bribery and bringing unaccounted money to England. But many of the committee members owned shares in the East India Company, and had themselves made fortunes from Clive's acquisition of Bengal. So when the matter was put to vote before the parliament, the majority of the members voted in Clive's favour!

But even in his success, Clive didn't find comfort. In 1774, he attempted suicide for a third time, and this time, he succeeded, losing a deeply personal battle with his own mind.

Clive was indeed a paradox. He harassed his schoolteachers, but worshipped his mentor in the army, Major Lawrence. He hated school, but educated himself in the Madras Library. He was a bold soldier, but he won his greatest battle by cunning manipulation. He had no qualms accepting all the wealth that came his way after the Battle of Plassey, but wanted to weed out corruption in the Company. He has been variously described as a military genius, a greedy speculator, an imperialist, an honourable English gentleman and more. Historians love him or loathe him, but all agree that Indian history would have been very different without Clive.

21

Ala-ud-din Khilji's Fort of Heads

SIRI FORT, DELHI

A king who hung the heads of thieves on a tower for all to see;
A tyrant, a fanatic and a brilliant general – this man was
all three!
A trusted lieutenant he gained as one of the many spoils of war,
His tower of victory was to be twice as tall as the Qutb Minar;
A powerful general who kept at bay the dreaded Mongol hordes –
He was one in a line of ruthless kings who lived and died by
the sword.

In the heart of south Delhi lie the ruins of a 14th-century fort called the Siri Fort. That in Urdu/Hindi literally means 'the fort of heads'. Legend has it that the then ruler of Delhi, Sultan Ala-ud-din Khilji, displayed on the walls of this very fort the heads of 8,000 men he had beheaded. If you are familiar with the name Ala-ud-din Khilji, you are perhaps picturing a ruthless tyrant and a religious fanatic. Why does he have that reputation and how much of it is true?

Ala-ud-din Khilji was the nephew and son-in-law of the Delhi sultan Jalal-ud-din Khilji, who ruled during the 13th–14th centuries. In 1296, the ambitious

Siri Fort ruins

Ala-ud-din assassinated his own uncle and then hoisted his severed head on a spear in full public sight. It was a loud statement and a sign of things to come. He crowned himself the king of Delhi and within a year, he killed, blinded or arrested everyone who was loyal to Jalal-ud-din's family, including courtiers who had supported him.

The new ruler of Delhi believed in ruling by complete intimidation. He quickly raised a powerful army, and began conquering and plundering neighbouring territories. By 1299, Ala-ud-din's commanders had conquered kingdoms as far as Gujarat, and brought back untold wealth to the capital. The loot from Gujarat included a particularly interesting asset: a transgender slave named Malik Kafur. He had a sharp mind and was every bit as ruthless as Ala-ud-din. The sultan took an immediate liking to Kafur and absorbed him in the army. The smart and capable Kafur rose quickly through the ranks and soon became a trusted general. He and Ala-ud-din Khilji made for a deadly combination, in both war and in politics.

In the early 1300s, Ala-ud-din sent Kafur on a campaign to southern India. Led by the shrewd Kafur, the soldiers easily conquered Deccan, and reached Madurai, the prosperous capital of the Pandya kingdom. The immensely rich Madurai Meenakshi Temple was plundered, and Kafur's troops returned to Delhi, carrying back vast treasures from there. This was the first time that a king from north India had scored such a resounding victory in the deep south.

Ala-ud-din meted out harsh punishments to those who dared to break the laws of his kingdom. Any merchant caught cheating had an equal weight of flesh cut off from his limbs. Thieves were quickly put to death. Their heads were displayed on a tower called the Chor Minar, which means 'the tower of thieves'. The tower still stands at a busy roundabout in Delhi.

His ruthlessness apart, Ala-ud-din was a brilliant general. His greatest accomplishment was to keep the Mongols out of India.

North India had long borne the brunt of Mongol raids – over a 100-year period from 1221 to 1327 – from the times of Genghis Khan. The nomadic Mongols were merciless invaders who wiped out entire cities and cultures, leaving a trail of utter devastation in their wake. They were originally from Mongolia, but by the late 13th century, their territories spanned large parts of Asia and Europe.

Ala-ud-din's predecessor, Jalal-ud-din had barely managed to fend off their attacks, but Ala-ud-din was more than a match for them. He was fully alert to this threat and prepared for it. He built new forts and repaired old ones. Permanent armies, led by trusted generals, were kept in readiness along the borders. And when the Mongols attacked, Ala-ud-din's army took them on and beat them back, not just once, but six times in a row. It is said that he once chased the retreating Mongols, beheaded thousands of them and displayed their heads on the walls of his fort. The fort came to be called 'Siri Fort' after this incident. So now you know why!

Chor Minar

During Jalal-ud-din's reign, some of the Mongols had converted to Islam and stayed back in Delhi as refugees, in an area that is to this day called 'Mangolpuri'. When his spies informed Ala-ud-din that some of these Mongols were conspiring to kill him, he massacred them all, wiping out nearly 30,000 Mongols in one fell swoop! Ala-ud-din did not believe in half measures; he met cruelty with more cruelty.

A common stereotype of Ala-ud-din Khilji projects him as a religious bigot. It is true that he imposed a special tax called *jizya* on the Hindus. But some historians view him more as an opportunist than a religious fanatic. He raided temples many a time, tempted by the wealth they contained.

Interestingly, he was not a pious Muslim either. He frequently skipped Friday prayers and often disregarded the ulema, the Islamic scholars. At the height of his success, it is believed that he even wanted to start his own religion! Ala-ud-din's unpopularity therefore transcended religious lines - neither the Muslims nor the Hindus liked him.

Despite doling out brutality in large measures, Ala-ud-din himself craved adulation. He considered himself a great conqueror and even called himself 'Sikander-i-Sani', or 'the next Alexander'. Like many megalomaniacs, he wanted to leave a lasting legacy, a grand monument. He commissioned the Alai Minar, a tower of victory that was to be twice as tall as the Qutb Minar. What better way to awe posterity! You can

Alai Darwaza

At the high point of his reign, Ala-ud-din decided to leave his mark in grand monuments. The unfinished Alai Minar still stands within the Qutb Minar complex. While it failed to give Ala-ud-din the fame he sought, another monument that he created within the same campus, the Alai Darwaza, did!

The Quwwat-ul-Islam Mosque in the Qutb Minar complex had already been in existence for over a century. Although Ala-ud-din was not an orthodox Muslim, he decided to win public recognition by adding four ornamental gateways around it. Only one of them, the Alai Darwaza was completed.

In many ways it is a remarkable structure and is considered one of the earliest examples of Indo-Islamic architecture in India. The dome on the structure is one of the earliest true domes seen on a monument on the Indian subcontinent. It is made of red sandstone and marble, and has beautiful *jaali* or latticed stonework windows, along with artistic calligraphy on the walls.

Alai Minar

still see the unfinished structure inside the Qutb Minar complex. But why wasn't it finished?

In the last years of his life, Ala-ud-din fell very sick. His slave-turned-partner, Malik Kafur, took over the throne. Ala-ud-din died in 1316, before the tower could be completed. Many historians believe he was killed by Malik Kafur, who then blinded Ala-ud-din's eldest son and imprisoned another one. But within a month, Malik himself was assassinated. The bloodbath didn't end there. Another of Ala-ud-din's sons took over as the king. Then, he too was murdered, ironically by his own trusted slave. And that was the end of the Khilji dynasty.

More than 600 years have passed and many kings and dynasties have followed the Khiljis. But the ruins of Siri Fort and Alai Minar continue to stand in Delhi – a reminder of a line of brutal kings who lived by the sword and died by it too.

22

The Delhi Durbar and the Imperial Crown of India

GATEWAY OF INDIA, MUMBAI

The city put on a spectacular show
When the royal couple came to town;
Kings in their finest queued up and bowed down
Though uneasy lay the head that wore the crown!
It was a gathering like none other, of mighty, powerful men –
Rulers of princely states, and some of the richest men
back then.

The year was 1911.

The British monarch, Edward VII, had died, and his son was due to be crowned. This was a time when the British king ruled over most of India. Even the remaining parts of India, comprising about 565 princely states, were indirectly controlled by resident British 'advisers'. India, at the time, was considered the 'jewel in the crown' of the British Empire, but no reigning British ruler had ever visited India before. And so the British decided to use this occasion to put on a spectacular show of power.

They planned to officially crown King George V as the Emperor of India at a grand ceremony in Delhi, but the unprecedented idea resulted in some unexpected challenges for the British in India.

To begin with, the Archbishop of Canterbury, the religious head of England who had to solemnize the coronation, refused to perform the sacred ceremony outside England. So it was decided that the crowning ceremony would be held in England in June 1911, followed by a 'durbar', or a formal reception, in India in December. The British officials in India saw this durbar as the ideal opportunity to bring all the Indian kings together to greet their monarch and acknowledge him as the Emperor of India.

The next hurdle came from an archaic British law, which held that the crown could never be taken overseas. This rule came from centuries earlier to safeguard the crown jewels from reckless kings who might have sold them off. So how were they to hold a Coronation Durbar without the crown?

There was a simple answer to that: to make a new crown, and have the 'India Office' pay for it! This department was set up in 1858 to supervise the English officials governing India. This meant that India, and not England, was paying for King George's new crown. The royal jewellers decided to splurge on the new crown and studded it with as many priceless gems as they could lay their hands on. The result was 'The Imperial Crown of India', with 6,170 diamonds, and many more emeralds, rubies and sapphires on it. It weighed over 900 grams, nearly a kilo! A matching tiara was made for Queen Mary.

Imperial Crown of India

Now came the trickiest part. The same British rule book dictated that no one else was allowed to wear a crown in the presence of the British monarch. This meant that the Indian kings had to be convinced to attend the ceremony without their beloved crowns, which were symbols of their lineage, pride and status. These kings were not nonentities by any measure. The Nizam of Hyderabad, for instance, was probably the richest man in the world at the time and the Maharaja of Baroda had a palace many times larger than Buckingham Palace! Convincing them that they could not wear their crowns at the Imperial Durbar wasn't going to be easy.

The British mulled over the issue and came up with a clever plan. They announced the durbar dress code: all royals would wear their ceremonial regalia with a traditional turban and '*sarpech*'. A *sarpech* is an ornament, often an exquisitely crafted piece made of expensive gemstones, pinned to the turban. It literally meant 'affixed to the head'. With that, the British managed to subtly ban crowns at this gathering. Meanwhile, the Indian royals brought out their finest turbans and sparkliest *sarpeches*. An awkward diplomatic incident had been smartly averted.

Preparations for the durbar cost over GBP 1 million, and Delhi was ready to receive about 12,000 VIPs and over 100,000 citizens. Meanwhile, in Bombay, where the royal ship was to dock, the British officials decided

Gateway of India

For anyone arriving by sea, the Gateway of India is one of the first visible Mumbai landmarks. While it was built a tad too late to welcome King George V to India, it has been witness to much history since then. This elegant monument is a wonderful fusion of Hindu, Islamic and European architectural styles. This blend of styles is called Indo-Saracenic, and it was a favourite of British architects of the period. George Wittet, the chief architect of this monument, used it extensively in Mumbai. The Prince of Wales Museum (now Chhatrapati Shivaji Maharaj Vastu Sangrahalaya), the Tata headquarters at Bombay House, The Grand Hotel, and many other landmark buildings in Ballard Estate were all built in the same style by Wittet. The main structure, made of yellow basalt, reminds one of Roman triumphal arches, but it is embellished with delicate lattice work on the arches, which is so typical of Indian architecture.

to build a majestic gateway commemorating the king's landing. The only problem was that they couldn't get the plan approved quickly enough. The Gateway of India was finally completed in 1924, thirteen years after King George V visited India! This beautiful basalt monument has stood there ever since. It was also the place from where the last of the British regiments left India forever, in 1948.

So just what did the British king and queen see when they got off their ships in Bombay? They saw a giant cardboard model of the gateway that the British officials had quickly raised for the occasion.

On 12 December 1911, King George V, wearing the Imperial Crown of India, sat with Queen Mary under an ornate canopy in Delhi. The event was held in north Delhi and 30 villages were cleared to create a temporary city built for thousands of guests and their entourage. The 'city' was complete with pathways, gardens, pavilions, dining rooms and amphitheatres. About 50,000 troops, cavalry, foot soldiers and artillery, were in attendance. Every royal invitee walked up to the emperor, bowed to him three times and cautiously walked backwards to their seats, without showing their backs to him. The durbar was a grand success.

Well, almost.

Delhi Durbar

The ceremonies had been rehearsed with all participants so that there would be no hitch. But the proud Maharaja of Baroda chose to ignore his instructions. When his turn came, he walked up to the emperor, merely nodded to him, turned and walked away, defiantly showing his back to the British monarch. The British press went berserk: How dare he! The maharaja later 'explained 'that he was so overawed by the occasion that he forgot the protocol. King George V underplayed the incident and later even knighted the maharaja.

While the Delhi Durbar did promote the feel-good factor, not everyone was impressed. The Maharaja of Mewar refused to attend the ceremony, because he had to pay obeisance to the English king. He reached Delhi for the ceremony in a special train, but then decided to turn around and head back from the railway station. His chair was conspicuously vacant in the VIP gallery. You can see this chair at the City Palace Museum in Udaipur even today. The euphoria from the gala event was also short-lived. The Indian freedom struggle was gathering steam and, four years after the durbar, a Gujarati lawyer named Mohandas Karamchand Gandhi landed in India after a long stint in South Africa, and went on to change everything for the British in India.

Twenty years after the Delhi Durbar, on 11 November 1931, King George V hosted a grand tea party for prominent Indian leaders at his residence, the Buckingham Palace. However, the mood of this 'durbar' was very different. These leaders had come to negotiate a bigger role for Indians in governing their own country. So there were no grandiose costumes and rituals, but there was definitely a formal European-style dress code. Mahatma Gandhi politely refused to comply with that code. He agreed to attend only if he would be allowed in his simple clothes. The royal office didn't really have a choice, and Gandhi arrived in his typical attire – khadi dhoti and Indian sandals, with a handwoven shawl wrapped around him to keep warm. His minimalistic style caused a sensation in London. It is said that a reporter earnestly asked him if he thought he was wearing enough to meet the king, arguably the world's most powerful man at the time. And Gandhi replied, with his trademark grin, that the king was wearing enough for the both of them!

The Delhi Durbar was a spectacular gala, and a successful one. What did it achieve? The gaiety of the durbar partly softened the public resentment that followed the Indian Rebellion of 1857. At the Durbar, King George announced the revocation of an earlier, unpopular order splitting up the Bengal Presidency. The resulting reunification won the hearts of many

Indians. He also announced a plan to shift the capital of the country from Calcutta to Delhi. The durbar was an extravagant and meticulously planned exercise to win the goodwill of the public.

After the durbar, the crown was taken back to England and placed along with the other royal jewels. It has never been worn since 1911. A diary note that King George V made on the night of the durbar is telling. The crown, he wrote, gave him a headache!

23

Colachel: The Battle that Ended the Dutch Ambitions in India

UDAYAGIRI FORT, THUCKALAY

The most powerful company in the whole wide world
Monopolized Kerala's spice trade with remarkable ease;
Until a 24-year-old king, fearless and bold,
Took away its privileges, brought it down to its knees!
Near the southern tip of India, a historic battle was fought
Between a small kingdom and a mighty colonial power;
It was the changes that this battle brought
That made the Dutch leave India forever.

Nestled in Kanniyakumari district, the southernmost tip of the Indian mainland, is the small town of Colachel. In 1741, this was the scene of a landmark battle; a battle that curtailed the ambitions of a mighty colonial power in India – the Dutch.

Like all other colonizing nations that came to India, the Dutch too arrived as traders. But by the late 17th century, the Dutch East India company or the Vereenigde Oostindische Compagnie (VOC), had grown from a mere trading institution to a naval and

Logo of the Vereenigde Oostindische Compagnie

economic superpower. It had a net worth higher than that of the top 20 multinational companies of today put together, and a strong military force at its disposal.

By this time, the Portuguese, who earlier had a monopoly over trade with the east, were gradually losing steam. The British were beginning to establish trading stations across India but were still small in comparison to the Dutch in both trade and military might. So the Dutch were well positioned to become the most dominant colonial power in India. A large part of their trade consisting of spices, which came from small south Indian kingdoms along the Malabar coast (in present-day Kerala). The VOC had signed one-sided contracts with most of these kingdoms, giving the Dutch the benefit as well as the monopoly over trading in spices with India. With this stranglehold over purchases, the Dutch dominated the world spice trade.

Things changed in 1729 when 24-year-old Anizham Tirunal Marthanda Varma ascended the throne of Travancore, a kingdom which included parts of present-day Kerala and southern Tamil Nadu. Over the next 30 years, he transformed Travancore from a tiny, nondescript kingdom into one of the richest and most powerful kingdoms in the history of Kerala. He conquered and annexed many of the smaller neighbouring kingdoms. Marthanda Varma was more powerful and ambitious than all the other local rulers. After he conquered these territories, Marthanda Varma flatly refused to comply with the unfair spice contracts with the Dutch. As a result, the VOC faced a sharp decline in pepper trade. Furthermore, Marthanda Varma's friendly relations with the British also added to their worries.

So, in 1739, the Dutch colonial governor, Gustaaf van Imhoff, met King Marthanda Varma and 'advised' him to restore Dutch trading privileges and respect the earlier treaties. The only other option was to prepare for war, he threatened. Marthanda Varma laughed it off and said that he rather liked the second idea, and would love to invade Holland himself!

Imhoff did not find it funny at all. When a small Indian kingdom boldly defied the world's biggest multinational company, it was bad for both business and image! In 1740, he dispatched a powerful naval contingent under the leadership of an officer named Eustachius De Lannoy to attack Travancore. De Lannoy, who had joined the Dutch East India company at a very young age, was a brilliant strategist and an expert in military fortifications. Under his command, the Dutch forces set sail to capture Padmanabhapuram, the capital of Travancore. They captured the coastal town of Colachel, which was just 13 km away from Padmanabhapuram and set up their base in the town. The Dutch infantry, artillery and navy were vastly superior. The Travancore army did have more troops, but at the time of the Dutch attack, they were engaged in military campaigns elsewhere. Therefore, in the initial battles the Dutch emerged victorious. Their armies advanced and they were all set to capture Padmanabhapuram. But, soon, the Travancore forces

Eustachius De Lannoy was not ethnically Dutch but belonged to an immigrant noble family from the Franco-Belgian border town of Lannoy. America's longest serving President, Franklin Delano Roosevelt, also descended from immigrants of the same De Lannoy family. Delano…De Lannoy… get the connection?

under the command of Marthanda Varma returned from the other campaigns. They put up a strong fight, forcing the Dutch to retreat to their base in Colachel.

Marthanda Varma knew that if he attacked Colachel outright, his army stood no chance against the Dutch artillery. Instead, he decided to blockade the Dutch post at Colachel from a safe distance and cut off their supplies. He calculated that if he held fast until the monsoons arrived, the sea would become too violent for Dutch supply ships to dock at Colachel. Without replenishments, the Dutch would either starve, or would have to break out and face the large Travancore army.

The strategy worked.

The monsoon rains pelted down and the Dutch struggled to keep their gunpowder dry. The wet season brought sickness and an epidemic broke out in the Dutch camp. And to top it all, a wildly lucky shot from a Travancore cannon landed smack on the Dutch armoury. Everything exploded, and all their ammunition was destroyed. That put an end to the Dutch resistance, and they were forced to surrender.

How did the technologically superior Dutch army lose to Travancore? Folklore is full of the military ploys Marthanda Varma practised to dissuade the Dutch fleet from landing on unguarded shores. He had sections of coconut tree trunks cut, painted black and installed on the beaches. From a distance at sea, the Dutch thought they were shore cannons. In the daytime, he had fishermen parading on the beaches with upturned oars – making them look like musketeers; and at night fishermen were asked to walk along the beach with burning torches, giving the impression that a large number of soldiers were regrouping on the shores. How much of this is true is anybody's guess, but Marthanda Varma was undoubtedly a master strategist, and in the Battle of Colachel, he clearly outwitted the Dutch.

What happened to De Lannoy and the Dutch soldiers? They were immediately stripped of their arms and imprisoned. But to everyone's surprise, Marthanda Varma offered them a way out. He asked them to join the Travancore army and fight on his side! He had seen the might of the Dutch forces and realized that his army could greatly benefit from their expertise. A handful of Dutch soldiers promptly joined the king's army – most notably, De Lannoy himself. He never returned to Holland and went on to serve Travancore loyally for 37 years.

De Lannoy worked tirelessly to modernize the Travancore army. He trained the army, upgraded the artillery and reinforced the forts. He soon won the king's confidence and rose to become Travancore's trusted general, or 'Valiya Kapittan', literally meaning 'Great Captain'. Travancore gradually expanded and went on to become one of the strongest kingdoms in south India. The Udayagiri Fort that De Lannoy rebuilt near Thiruvananthapuram is still called 'Dillanai Kotta', the local way of saying 'De Lannoy's Fort'.

Marthanda Varma shared a deep personal relationship with his favourite captain as well. When De Lannoy fell in love with a local widow of Portuguese descent, the Maharaja exercised his royal influence to convince her reluctant father to allow their marriage. He even sponsored a Catholic church inside the fort and paid the Vicar's salary. Later, De Lannoy's only son also joined the Travancore army, but was killed in action when he was barely twenty. De Lannoy continued to live in the Udayagiri Fort and serve Marthanda Varma until he died of illness in 1777. He was buried in the Catholic chapel in the fort with full honours.

The Battle of Colachel was a minor battle in military terms, but it was a major turning point for several reasons. This was the first time that an Indian kingdom had defeated a European naval force. The Dutch were thoroughly demoralized by the defeat. They continued to fight Marthanda Varma for a few more years, but with indifferent results. After all, the king was already familiar with their methods! Moreover, the Dutch had lost access to Kerala's spices, and the economic impact was immense. Finally, they signed a peace treaty with Marthanda Varma.

They gradually shifted their base to Indonesia, which was another spice-rich country and ultimately left India forever. And with that, the British East India Company became the largest European military power in India.

THIS PILLAR
COMMEMORATES
THE VICTORY OF
THE TRAVANCORE
ARMY
OVER THE DUTCH
AT COLACHAL ON
THE
31ST JULY 1741A.D

Victory Pillar

The southernmost tip of the Indian mainland is called Kanniyakumari (earlier Cape Comorin). It is a pilgrimage and tourist centre. About 38 km to the north-west is the historic town of Colachel, a busy fishing harbour with a lovely beach. The town celebrates 31 July every year as Colachel Day, for, it was on this day in 1741 that the Dutch forces surrendered to Marthanda Varma's army. A victory pillar commemorates the historic event. Padmanabhapuram (Marthanda Varma's capital) and Udayagiri Fort (which became De Lannoy's stronghold) are both within 15 km of Colachel. From Kanniyakumari, one can make a short daytrip covering all three protected monuments – Colachel Pillar, Padmanabhapuram Palace and Udayagiri Fort.

24

The Englishman Who Showed Indians the Power of a Free Press

HORNIMAN CIRCLE, MUMBAI

There's a charming green circle, a wide, open space
In the heart of bustling Mumbai, its most prime address;
It's named after an Englishman who made this his base
And showed Indians the might and power of a free press.
A champion of civil liberty, he gave a strong voice
To the subdued and neglected Indian point of view;
The British shipped him out, but then had no choice –
When he came back by train, they had to let him through!

In the heart of Mumbai's busy financial district is a charming circle with a park in the centre, and bordered by fine colonial-era buildings. It is the Zero Point of Mumbai, from where all distances to and from the city are measured. In the early 1800s, this area was a fortified settlement of the British. The St Thomas Cathedral, which was built within the fort walls over 300 years ago, still stands at one end of the park. It was then called Elphinstone Circle, after Lord Elphinstone, under whose governorship the area was developed.

By the mid-1800s, Fort George, the British fort in Bombay, had outlived its purpose. The British decided to raze the fort walls to make more space for their growing settlement. That open ground, called Bombay Green, quickly turned into a waste dump. So the British decided to transform the area into a planned urban development, the very first of its kind in Bombay. They cleared the debris and planted trees. Walkways were paved and a fountain was installed in the centre. Its design was inspired by the Park Crescent in London, and soon Elphinstone Circle became a sought-after commercial area. The landmarks around the Horniman Circle Gardens include the magnificent Town Hall, which houses the Asiatic Society of Mumbai, and the St Thomas Cathedral, the oldest Anglican church in Mumbai.

Horniman Circle

After the British left in 1947, many landmarks began to be renamed after Indian leaders and heroes, but Elphinstone Circle was an exception. It was renamed as Horniman Circle, in memory of another Englishman, Benjamin Horniman. This is his story.

By the turn of the 20th century, numerous protests against British occupation were erupting in small towns and cities across India. These were spontaneous protests of an oppressed people disconnected from the larger freedom movement, so the British were able to suppress them easily and could keep them confined to small pockets. They even made sure that news about these did not spread much. After all, they controlled most of the English-language newspapers in India. The British had the power to censor and suppress dissenting views. As a result, Indians were often unaware of what was happening in the other parts of their own country.

This was a sore point with Indian nationalists. They wanted to spread awareness of the freedom movement and unite Indians under a common banner of protest. But most English newspapers of the time ignored Indian aspirations. So, in 1910, Sir Pherozeshah Mehta, a prominent lawyer who had also served as president of the Indian National Congress in 1890, decided to start his own English newspaper. He called it the *Bombay Chronicle*. He wanted an independent-minded editor to run this newspaper and found him in an Englishman named Benjamin Guy Horniman.

Horniman was an experienced journalist who, from a young age, had been fascinated by India. After writing for several newspapers in Britain, he came to Calcutta in 1906, and joined *The Statesman* as a news editor. In the wake of the partition of Bengal in 1905 and the subsequent rioting and violence across the state, Horniman had covered these happenings fearlessly and impartially, pulling up the British Indian Government for its callous attitude towards Indians. He had made a name for himself as a champion of civil liberty.

Benjamin Guy Horniman

At the *Bombay Chronicle* too, Horniman continued to give voice to the Indian viewpoint. British officials at the highest levels were often at the receiving end of his honest and scathing articles. His efforts won the hearts of many Indians, including Mahatma Gandhi and other leaders of the freedom movement. Naturally, he had only a few friends among the British bureaucracy in India. The British establishment waited for the right opportunity to silence him. That opportunity came in 1919.

On 13 April 1919, a crowd of unarmed people had gathered to protest peacefully against the British at a public ground called Jallianwala Bagh in Amritsar, Punjab. The British troops opened fire on them without provocation. More than 1,650 rounds were fired; at least 379 Indians died and over 1,200 were injured. This included men, women and even children. It was a major human rights violation and the British realized that the repercussions would be disastrous for them. So the local administrators decided on a quick cover-up. They imposed martial law in Punjab, stifled the press and censored all news about the massacre. Unfortunately for them, a local correspondent named Lala Govardhan Das managed to write a detailed eyewitness account of the incident, and Horniman published every gory detail in the *Bombay Chronicle*. News of this shocking incident spread across India, and Horniman's words threatened to destabilize the government. The British acted swiftly.

They immediately jailed Govardhan Das and quietly deported Horniman back to England. That, in hindsight, wasn't a very smart move. Horniman took with him all the evidence he had collected about the Jallianwala Bagh incident. On reaching England, he wasted no time in publishing the images and articles in the *Daily Herald* newspaper. The British public, which until then was largely unexposed to the harsh realities of colonial rule, was horrified by the news. There was public outrage and the opposition party raised a furore. Over the next seven years, Horniman continued to expose the misdemeanours of the British and even published a book that was a severe denunciation of British rule in India. The British Indian government officially banned the distribution of these papers in India, but Horniman cleverly smuggled clippings to India through friends and these were republished in the *Bombay Chronicle*.

Horniman was still determined to return to India. In 1926, he decided to exploit a loophole in his deportation order, which explicitly stated that he was not allowed to land in India. So Horniman took a long-winded route. He sailed from the UK to Colombo, from where he boarded a train to Bombay. When produced before a magistrate, he respectfully pointed out that he hadn't broken any rules. He had come by train, so he had not 'landed' but merely 'alighted' in India. The court had to let him go on this technicality.

Horniman rejoined the *Bombay Chronicle* and continued his crusade. In time, he began his own newspapers, such as the *Indian National Herald* and the

Bombay Sentinel. The focus of all his writing was to make India a better place for Indians. But he didn't stop with just writing. He became an active participant in the ongoing freedom movement. He joined Mahatma Gandhi in his protest against the infamous Rowlatt Act of 1919, which allowed the British authorities to put Indians on trial without juries and imprison suspects without trial. He also served as the vice president of the Home Rule Movement started by his compatriot, Annie Besant. Horniman kept the British on tenterhooks with his caustic pen and his clear anti-colonial vision. That endeared him to the local population. He remained a central figure in journalistic circles until Indian independence. He died in 1948.

Horniman's best days were with the *Bombay Chronicle.* In those days the newspaper functioned from the Bombay Samachar building at Elphinstone Circle. In 1948, after Horniman's death, the circle was renamed 'Horniman Circle' in honour of the Englishman who showed Indians the power of a free press.

The *Bombay Samachar* (now *Mumbai Samachar*) is a Gujarati newspaper that was started in 1822 and is still running after nearly 200 years. It is the oldest functioning newspaper in all of Asia. Its offices are down a nondescript alley just off Horniman Circle.

Amidst all the imposing structures at Horniman Circle, there is also an old banyan tree that made history. If you walk into the Horniman Circle Gardens, you will find a drinking-water booth called a *pyau*. Such kiosks were commonly donated by philanthropists as a service to thirsty passers-by. In the 1850s people came for a drink of water and enjoyed a short break under the shade of the adjoining banyan tree. Soon that tree became a place for business networking. Among the people who gathered under the tree everyday was a small group of sharebrokers who met there to conduct business. Soon that group of brokers formed a business association that grew to become the Bombay Stock Exchange, Asia's oldest stock exchange. Money does grow under trees!

25

Measuring the Height of Mount Everest

ST THOMAS MOUNT, CHENNAI

Many pioneering men gave their blood, sweat and tears
To this monumental effort that took over 70 long years –
A survey that mapped and measured a vast expanse of land
And identified the tallest of all tall mountains that stand.

They braved dense forests, deep rivers and cliffs that were sheer
And ended up proving that Earth is not a perfect sphere.
In the heat and rain, it was courage they displayed –
This was the largest measurement of Earth's surface ever made!

How did they map this land, measure the height of hills?
Simple, they used their trigonometrical skills!
It is well known that Mt Everest is tall
And it is this survey that identified it as the tallest peak of all!

Mount Everest is the tallest peak on Earth. It is named after Sir George Everest, a British surveyor and geographer. Strangely, George Everest was not the man who identified it as the world's tallest peak. In fact, he never visited or surveyed Mount Everest in his lifetime. So why is the peak named after him? Come to think

At 8,849 m (29,032 ft), Mt Everest is the tallest peak on Earth, measured from the mean sea level. But if you measure from the base of the mountain, Mauna Kea in Hawaii is the tallest. That is because its base is under the sea and its height from the sea floor is 10,211 m!

of it, how did anyone determine that Everest was the tallest peak in the world? The answers are hidden in a remarkable project carried out under the British: the Great Trigonometrical Survey of India.

It was a project that took over 70 years to complete. A reminder of this monumental effort can be seen at St Thomas Mount in Chennai. This is the site where the Apostle, St Thomas, is believed to have been martyred nearly 2,000 years ago. Just outside the shrine, there is a less well-known monument, completely unrelated to Christianity. There, under a tree, sits the bust of a British soldier and geographer, Colonel William Lambton, who headed the Great Trigonometrical Survey of India. In 1802, it was from here that Lambton launched his fieldwork for a survey that went on to span the length and breadth of the entire subcontinent. What prompted him to do that?

By the end of the 18th century, the British East India Company (EIC) had annexed vast territories in India and indirectly controlled many princely states too. Now that the British had control over so much land, they had

A bust of Col Lambton

to mark their territory, create political boundaries and invest in infrastructure. For this, they needed accurate maps of the land. The existing maps were reasonable approximations at best and often unscientific. William Lambton, then a major in the army, suggested that they embark on a complete survey of India to map the entire country precisely. Lambton was a passionate astronomer and had even lost an eye while intensely observing a solar eclipse. The EIC was initially reluctant, but eventually accepted the idea and made Lambton the project leader.

Lambton decided to use the tools of trigonometry for the project. Trigonometry (Greek for the science of triangle measurement) was developed by ancient Egyptian, Greek, Arab and Indian mathematicians and was a mature science by that time. Specifically, Lambton relied on a methodology called 'triangulation'. Essentially, it means that if you know the distance between any two points on a line (called a baseline), you can accurately calculate the distance to a third point from the baseline, using a trigonometric formula, *without physically measuring that distance*. You only need to measure the angles between the two ends of the baseline and the third point. These three points would form a triangle of land. And you can keep adding more adjacent triangles to that to map any large area.

On 10 April 1802, Lambton fixed flagpoles at two points in Madras, now Chennai: one at Marina Beach and the other at the grandstand of the Madras racecourse, nearly 6 km away. This 'baseline' was measured using a 100-foot-long steel chain.

Lambton supervising triangulation

Next, he proceeded to measure the angles between the two ends of the baseline and the top of St Thomas Mount, a hillock nearby. For this, he used an instrument called the 'theodolite', to measure angles. With that data in hand, he could now precisely calculate the distance and height of St Thomas Mount, using trigonometric formulae.

A theodolite

More importantly, he could now use that new distance as a baseline of an adjacent triangle, to calculate the distance to another point even further away.

So, armed with heavy measuring instruments and a team of 150 men, Lambton set out on foot, going from hill to hill, taking measurements. The special steel chain that Lambton used was exactly 100 feet long. But since steel could expand or contract with temperature, thermometer readings were taken at every instance and calculations were adjusted for thermal expansion! The theodolite alone weighed half a tonne and needed 12 people to carry it. He used another instrument called the 'zenith sector' for determining the location of a site with reference to the stars. Every measurement that the team took was adjusted for the curvature of Earth, altitude and other variations. It was a slow, painstaking method, but Lambton never compromised on quality.

Nearly four years later, they reached the Mangalore coast that lay some 580 km away. Lambton had succeeded in calculating the distance between the east and west coast of south India with extraordinary accuracy. He was now encouraged to extend the survey to cover the entire subcontinent. Two more phases were planned; the southern phase from Kanniyakumari to Nagpur, and the northern phase from Nagpur to Banog in the Himalayan foothills.

Lambton immediately set out with a large team to Kanniyakumari, on yet another adventurous journey. They walked over inhospitable terrain, faced torrential rains, mosquitoes, injuries and disease. Occasionally, they would face hostile rulers who had to be convinced that their team was not a military expedition but a scientific project. Once, Lambton's theodolite was captured by

In the European political scenario of the time, the French and British were often enemies. So, it is not surprising that the French seized the 'suspicious' looking package containing the theodolite from the British group. Ironically, the French recognized Lambton's work even before the British did. The French Institute in Paris elected him as a member, through its Science Academy, in 1817. Lambton was made Fellow of the (British) Royal Society only in 1818!

the French. When they understood the mission, they gracefully repacked and returned it.

Often, the survey team climbed hilltops and temple towers to get vantage viewpoints. Sometimes they constructed stone or mud towers specifically for this purpose.

Hundreds of mud and stone towers were built across the subcontinent to be used as reference points for the survey. Many of these still stand, nearly 200 years after they were constructed. You can see a bust of Lambton atop St Thomas Mount, where he started the survey, and a memorial called Kala Gota in Nagpur, where he finally rested. One hill in the Nilgiris Range is named Lambton Peak. Lambton's legacy can also be observed in Pakistan, Bangladesh, Nepal, Afghanistan, Bhutan and Myanmar. The database and technique to develop detailed maps that Lambton has created is used even today by cartographers in these South Asian countries.

On one occasion the theodolite was carefully hauled atop the 1,000-year-old Brihadeeswara Temple of Thanjavur (in Tamil Nadu), then the tallest temple in India. Unfortunately, the team accidentally dropped the heavy instrument from a height of 65 m! It took a long time to repair and re-deploy. Worse still, on its way down, the theodolite had shattered an ancient bas-relief on the temple tower, and Lambton was obliged to repair it. Even today, amidst all the murals and sculptures – which depict different scenes and stories from the Puranas – adorning the temple tower, one odd bas-relief depicts a man with distinctly European looks, wearing a top hat. It is believed that this was the handiwork of Lambton's repair team.

After 13 years of walking and mapping about 4,28,230 sq. km, they reached Hyderabad, 1,100 km from Kanniyakumari. It was here, in 1818, that a bright young deputy, Captain George Everest, joined the team. The team now proceeded towards Nagpur, the final stop before they would embark on their northern survey.

By this time, Lambton was nearly 70 years old. In 1823, he contracted tuberculosis and soon passed away. Everest, his deputy, assumed charge. He not only maintained Lambton's high standards, but also refined the team's techniques and tools. He completed the northern phase at Mussoorie in 1841, and retired in 1843.

Large chunks of territory remained unchartered. The responsibility of surveying these fell on Everest's deputy, Andrew Waugh. He pushed the survey to the Himalayas in the Nepalese and Tibetan territories. Both borders were closed to outsiders, so they were content to survey what they could see from across the border. The peaks of Nanda Devi and Kanchenjunga were measured for the very first time.

In 1847, they found a peak that appeared to be taller than all the others. They named it Peak XV. Radhanath Sikdar, the chief mathematician in the team at Calcutta office, checked the readings and found proof in 1852 that Peak XV was indeed the tallest peak in the world. Waugh was sceptical at first. But after several reviews over many years, he confirmed the discovery.

Waugh decided to name the peak after his illustrious predecessor and mentor, Sir George Everest. Everest felt a little embarrassed, and he wanted it called by the local name. But since the team could not enter Tibet or Nepal where the mountain actually stood, they could not confirm its local name. So, in 1865, the Royal Geographic Society accepted Waugh's recommendation and Peak XV was named Mount Everest.

Among the institutions established by the British in India, such as the universities, the courts, the railways and the bureaucracy, the Great Trigonometrical Survey was less glamorous but equally, if not more, remarkable. It was the largest measurement of Earth's surface ever attempted, and achieved astonishing accuracy, by sheer physical effort and pen-and-paper calculations. Even Lambton's parent country Britain was not mapped to the extent India was.

The survey covered an arc of longitude on Earth's surface from Kanniyakumari to the foothills of the Himalayas. It was named the Great Indian Arc of the Meridian and, among other things, it proved that Earth is not a perfect sphere but shaped like a grapefruit – an oblate spheroid. Scientists like Newton had long theorized about this, but Lambton's Trigonometric Survey gave irrefutable and accurate empirical evidence

An ellipsoid is somewhat like a sphere except that it may be longer in one or more dimensions. Rugby balls and eggs are good examples of this. An oblate spheroid is one kind of ellipsoid. It is like a ball that has been squashed at the top and bottom. The circumference around Earth's poles is therefore less than the circumference around the equator. In 1687, Newton had observed that Earth is an oblate spheroid because it rotates. The degree of flattening at either end depends on a planet's density, gravity and centrifugal force. Since this varies from planet to planet, some like Jupiter and Saturn are even more 'squashed'.

Oblate spheroid

of this. Today, the Survey of India (which absorbed the Great Trigonometrical Survey later) survives as one of the oldest Indian government departments.

While Lambton and Everest did not see the northern tip of India, the legacy they left behind is truly of Himalayan proportions.

26

The Misnamed Monuments of Mamallapuram

MAMALLAPURAM

For centuries the 'Butterball' has simply stood still —
It's famous as the rock that refuses to roll down the hill;
Then there is the monolith with some strange ironies
in its name —
A temple built for Lord Shiva is now Ganesha's chariot,
they claim;
The magnificent monuments of Mamallapuram have many
stories to tell,
Though their names often confound even those who know the
stories well!
At Mamallapuram, you can see these stories carved on
rock faces —
Every place has its story they say, but every story also lives
in a myriad of places.

About 60 km south of Chennai, along the coast of the Bay of Bengal, is the ancient seaside town of Mamallapuram. Ptolemy, the Greek scholar, wrote about this town as early as 140 CE, referring to it as Malange. Back then, Mamallapuram was a busy port.

Roman traders came here and so did the Chinese – all trading in pearls, gemstones and ivory.

In its heyday, in the seventh and eighth centuries, Mamallapuram was the atelier of the Pallavas, their stone workshop. It echoed with the sounds of chisels and mallets, as sculptors went about turning massive granite boulders into the finest works of art. The Pallavas were a powerful dynasty that ruled parts of present-day Tamil Nadu between the third and the ninth centuries. And in those 600-odd years, temple building in south India underwent a dramatic change. It is at Mamallapuram that sculptors began to experiment with various methods of

Historians believe that the Pallavas were feudatories of the Satavahana kings, who ruled over areas around modern-day Andhra Pradesh and Maharashtra up to the third century. The Pallavas ruled over parts of present-day northern Tamil Nadu, Andhra Pradesh and Karnataka between the third and the ninth centuries. Their capital was Kanchipuram, very close to Mamallapuram. They were at the peak of their power in the seventh and eighth centuries. That was the time when the land was ruled by three great Pallava kings – Mahendra Varman I, Narasimha Varman I and Narasimha Varman II. They were great patrons of art, literature and architecture. Much of the stonework you see in Mamallapuram was started during the rule of Mahendra Varman I in the late sixth century and came to an abrupt end when Narasimha Varman II died in the early eighth century.

handling stone, and at Mamallapuram, you can see the evolution of the Pallava style of temple architecture.

Initially, the Pallava masons simply carved designs on rock faces. Such structures are called bas-reliefs and the most famous one is the richly carved Arjuna's Penance. It is believed to be the largest open-air bas-relief in the world.

Arjuna's Penance bas-relief

It depicts an emaciated man, standing by a river in a posture of prayer. He is surrounded by creatures ranging from life-sized elephants to mice, men and gods. The natural cleft in between the two boulders has been cleverly woven into the sculpture, and represents a river. It is believed that this bas-relief depicts a story from the Hindu epic, Mahabharata, where the Pandava prince Arjuna prays to Lord Shiva for a magical weapon called the Pashupatastra.

At one point in the epic, the Pandavas lose their kingdom to their cousins, the Kauravas, in a gambling match. Not just that, they are banished from their own kingdom and exiled for 13 long years. One of these five brothers is Arjuna, a skilled archer. He decides to use the period of exile to hone his skills and upgrade his weaponry. He has his eyes set on a particular magical weapon called the Pashupatastra, the most powerful weapon in the universe. However, the weapon is held in the safe custody of Shiva, the god of destruction, and likely to be given only to a very deserving candidate. Arjuna, eager to qualify for it, sits and prays long and hard to Shiva. After a challenging penance, Shiva gifts him the Pashupatastra, a weapon so powerful that if used indiscriminately, it could destroy the entire world.

What does Arjuna do with it? Nothing. As they say, with great power comes great responsibility. Arjuna plans to use the Pashupatastra only when driven by extreme necessity. He goes on to fight the mother of all battles, facing many, many challenges, and yet never once does he use the Pashupatastra. The mere possession of the weapon proves to give him a psychological edge, and that confidence propels him to victory. His side eventually wins the war. And thus by practising restraint, he proves himself worthy of being bestowed with so much power.

On the bas-relief, the man deep in prayer, is assumed to be Arjuna. You can also see Shiva granting him the boon, while the other gods look on in admiration. This bas-relief does seem like a perfect depiction of this story from the Mahabharata, until you pay heed to other scholars who insist that it is not Arjuna from the

Mahabharata, but Bhagiratha, Rama's ancestor in the epic, Ramayana!

The story goes that a long time ago, there lived a king called Bhagiratha, who was desperate to complete the last rites of his ancestors according to Hindu customs. His forefathers who belonged to the Ikshvaku dynasty, all 60,000 of them, had died as a result of a curse and their ashes were scattered over a vast area. Their souls could ascend into heaven only if their ashes were immersed in the holy waters of Ganga. But back then, the Ganga flowed not on land but in the heavens. So Bhagiratha meditated and prayed hard to Lord Shiva. After years of penance, Shiva granted his boon and ordered Ganga to flow down to earth. But Ganga wasn't too pleased with this command and decided to descend down to earth with such force that it would throw the world off course. So Shiva stepped in to take the full force of Ganga's descent, trapped the waters in his long hair, and then gently released it to the earth. The river flowed over the ashes of Bhagiratha's ancestors, thus completing the ritual. Looking at the details on the bas-relief, it is not difficult to interpret it as the story of the 'Descent of the Ganga'.

So, does this bas-relief depict an event from the Mahabharata or from the Ramayana? Scholars haven't come to an agreement yet, and hence the monument goes by two names: 'Arjuna's Penance' and 'The Descent of the Ganga'.

This ambiguity in naming is seen in other monuments too in Mamallapuram. India is rich in monuments, and richer still in mythology. Sometimes the two together confound even informed Indians. The Ramayana and Mahabharata are the most famous Indian epics. Over the centuries, these highly popular epics have been narrated, written and rewritten ever so often, and have spawned many sequels, prequels and quaint regional variants, all rooted in the local lore. So it is not uncommon to find places scattered across India that draw a connection with these epics in different ways.

The most popular misnomer in Mamallapuram is a cluster of five unfinished structures known as 'Pancha Pandava Rathas,' or the 'Chariots of the Five Pandavas'. This monument is a monolith. It was part of the second stage in the evolution of Pallava temple-building techniques. It involved working on one huge rock, cutting out all the extra bits to leave a temple-like structure behind. The sculptors chose large blocks of granite, started chipping away the stone from the top and chiselled their way down, to create what is called a rock-cut temple. Monoliths need precise calculations and sculpting skills. One false move and the whole rock would be wasted. You can still see several half-finished monoliths scattered around Mamallapuram.

Each of the five rathas is different from the others. But they are all carved from a single rock that is connected below the surface. Each is now symbolically associated with one of the Pandavas. And there is one for Draupadi – the wife of the five Pandava brothers. The two youngest Pandava twins share the last ratha.

The Five Rathas

So what is the connection between the Pandavas and these structures? If the sculptors actually meant to depict them as the chariots of the five Pandavas, we have no evidence of it. At some point, they began to be associated with the five brothers and began to be called the Pancha Pandava Rathas.

There is even a 'Pancha Pandava Cave', and the folklore goes that the Pandavas sought shelter here, hiding during their exile. The legend is so ingrained that even archaeologists call it the Pancha Pandava Cave. They are among the earliest cave temples to be constructed in the Pallava Empire. To make the cave temple, sculptors had to gouge out the insides of a granite rock to create a cave, which could then be used to house a statue of a god. Soon this style became the norm. Masons scooped out great chunks of rock from hillsides and created fine cave temples.

Not all landmarks of Mamallapuram were built by the Pallavas. In the heart of the Mamallapuram complex is a gigantic round rock. At first glance in the shimmering heat of day, it almost seems to be floating, because the rock is enormous, and it sits on a ridiculously small and slippery base. It is 6 m tall, weighs over 250 tonnes and has been sitting there for over 1,200 years at least. It is balanced on an incline that should really push it over. Yet, this rock that refuses to roll. Legend goes that this rock is actually hardened butter! Lord Krishna, as a child, loved to steal dollops of butter and eat it on the sly. One large handful of the stolen butter fell there and hardened to become this very rock – or so goes the story. And that's why it is still called 'Krishna's Butterball'.

Another monolith at Mamallapuram that seems intriguingly named is the 'Ganesha Ratha'.

Ratha means a chariot, and this massive rock is clearly not a chariot. Nor was this temple originally

Ganesha Ratha

dedicated to Ganesha. It was a Shiva temple and had a *shivalinga* inside. Over time, the *shivalinga* was lost. So, some decades ago, local villagers decided to install a Ganesha idol inside. The temple has been called the Ganesha Ratha ever since.

But not all monuments in Mamallapuram are misnamed. Some, like the Olakaneswara temple, a temple to Lord Shiva, built on a hillock in the eighth century, have wonderfully apt names. It is believed that this hillock functioned as a lighthouse way back in the seventh century. Olakaneswara is another name for Shiva. It means the one with flaming eyes – a very fitting name for a lighthouse, don't you think? This structure is believed to be the oldest lighthouse in India.

Another monument with the perfect name is the Shore Temple.

Shore Temple

The Shore Temple is not a single temple, but a complex of three shrines. There were probably more temples here because one of the colonial names of Mamallapuram was Seven Pagodas – meaning 'seven temples'. Some historians believe that the other pagodas lie submerged somewhere along this coastline, but others disagree. This complex has two shrines for Shiva on either side and a Vishnu shrine sandwiched in between. The Shiva shrines were built around the early eighth century. The Vishnu shrine is thought to be older, built in the seventh century.

It has stood on these shores for nearly 1,300 years, and has featured in the accounts of many seafarers. This structure marked an important evolutionary step in temple building. Until then, bas-reliefs, monoliths and cave temples could be built only where huge rocks were available. By the late eighth century, building techniques had evolved to a stage where massive rocks could be moved and stacked, one over the other. So, then, a king could build his temples wherever he pleased. And the temple structures could be much taller than any individual piece of rock. The Shore Temple is considered the pinnacle of temple architecture in Mamallapuram. For this temple, the sculptors brought in cut rocks and expertly assembled them into a temple. One of the earliest structural temples in south India, it is not a very tall structure, but it is this little temple that became the prototype of many of the largest temples you can see in Tamil Nadu today. By the time of the later Cholas in the 10th century, temples with 100-foot-tall towers were fairly common in Tamil Nadu.

But why were all these structures built? And why do many of them have names that don't really match up? We don't know, because many of them were left incomplete. Perhaps they were made because in the seventh century, the Pallavas were experimenting with stone. Scholars believe that many of these monuments were never used as places of worship. For a temple to be consecrated, it has to have a finial – a lotus-bud shaped structure installed right at the very top. And in some of these monuments, you will find those placed on the floor, just near the monument. Were these temples never consecrated or were the finials brought down by invading armies? Sadly, we do not have definitive answers for many such questions. What we do have are many colourful myths that do a wonderful job of filling the gaps and sparking our imagination.

27

The Myths and Mysteries of the Big Temple

BRIHADEESWARA TEMPLE, THANJAVUR

A marvel of engineering, over a thousand years old,
This ancient temple has many secrets to unfold;
Made of hard granite, not marble, nor gold –
The magnum opus of a king who was astute and bold;
Sixteen storeys high, sixty-six metres tall,
It surely is 'big' – its name says it all!

A visit to the city of Thanjavur in Tamil Nadu would be incomplete without a visit to the 'Periya Kovil', as the locals call it. Periya Kovil literally translates to 'Big Temple' and, indeed, this is a huge temple. It was built as far back as 1010 CE, making it over a thousand years old! At the time it was built, it was the tallest man-made structure in the world, barring the pyramids in Egypt and Meso America. It is also called the Brihadeeswara Temple. Incidentally, 'Brihad' in Sanskrit also means 'big' or 'mighty', and this tall temple still awes its visitors as an engineering marvel, a millennium after it was built.

For centuries millions of devotees had come and admired this massive structure, strangely, without even knowing its real name. No one knew who built it or when. Then, in 1887, a German Indologist named Dr Eugen Hultzsch decided to find answers to this old puzzle. Hultzsch adored India and had devoted his life to decoding ancient Indian inscriptions. At that time, he was the chief epigraphist of the Archaeological Survey of India. He was supported by a brilliant assistant named Valaiyattur Venkayya, who had studied classical Indian languages. Moreover, he had access to the innermost parts of temples, which were out of bounds to Europeans like Hultzsch.

This pair noticed that all around the base of the main shrine were pretty little squiggles that, on first look, seemed mostly decorative. Venkayya would diligently copy down all the designs he saw on the walls inside and, together, they would try to interpret them. Soon they discovered that the squiggles were in fact inscriptions written in an ancient Tamil script that was very different from the modern Tamil script – and what a find that was!

It was only after the script was deciphered that the world got to know that this temple was built by a Chola king named Rajaraja. It was also found that the temple was originally called Rajarajeswaram. Rajaraja had thoughtfully left inscriptions on the temple walls, giving a detailed description of the temple's assets. He had literally carved his name in stone, and yet it remained undiscovered for centuries.

Brihadeeswara Temple

The story of the Big Temple is closely linked to the story of Rajaraja Chola who, as we know now, was one of the greatest Chola kings. He was crowned in 985 CE. The Chola kingdom at that time was a large territory in central Tamil Nadu. Rajaraja was strong, ambitious and determined to leave a mark on history.

Within a short span of time, he had subjugated the Pandyas of southern Tamil Nadu, the Cheras of Kerala and the Eastern Chalukyas of Andhra Pradesh, bringing much of the southern peninsula under Chola rule. Then, his navy conquered the northern half of Sri Lanka and the Maldives. Later, his son, Rajendra Chola, completed the conquest of southern Sri Lanka too,

Rajaraja Chola became king by accident. His elder brother Aditya Chola was the official heir to the kingdom, but was mysteriously assassinated in 969 CE. Popular sentiment was in favour of Rajaraja ascending the throne. But, surprisingly, Rajaraja stepped aside for his uncle Uttama Chola to take over the reins, because he was the eldest in the clan. Was it family love, or political astuteness? We will never know. Uttama Chola ruled for 15 years with Rajaraja quietly assisting him. When Uttama Chola died in 985 CE, Rajaraja became king. And that step up brought about an explosive change in Rajaraja too; the previously docile Rajaraja came into his own and quickly transformed into an ambitious, aggressive and astute ruler.

taking the mighty Chola empire to its greatest heights. The Chola coffers were overflowing and, soon, Rajaraja began commissioning grand temples and works of art. The one that was closest to his heart was the Big Temple of Thanjavur.

It is not uncommon for ancient temples in India to get woven into local folklore and to spawn many myths. The Big Temple is no exception, with its many incredible myths and mysteries. It is said that the *vimana*, or the main temple tower, never casts a shadow on earth! How can a 16-storey tall *vimana*, made of thousands of tonnes of solid granite, not cast a shadow? But a visit to the temple on any evening offers enough evidence that this is nothing more than a myth. As one might expect, the tall *vimana* does cast a long shadow.

A related question that has puzzled architects and historians for a long time is how the artisans hauled up all that granite a thousand years ago when there were no cranes or forklifts. The idol inside the temple is much larger than the temple doorway, so how then did they take the idol inside? It is believed that the temple has many secret passages. Where do they lead to and what secrets do they hide? Let's explore some of these myths and mysteries.

Rajaraja wanted the Big Temple to be the most magnificent of all temples and set extremely challenging goals for his engineers and artisans. His temple had to be unique, one that reflected his own power as much as the power of the god inside. So everything in this temple was designed to echo this. The *vimana* is 66 m tall, a feat that no one had achieved until then. All 16 levels of the *vimana* are made of solid granite, a heavy and very hard stone. As a rule, only the lower storeys of most temples are made of granite, with the others being made of lighter brick and stucco to help reduce the weight of the structure.

Rajaraja insisted his temple would be made entirely of stone, a material that would speak of his glory long after he was gone. The main idol inside the shrine is a massive *shivalinga* carved out of a single stone, and it is nearly two storeys tall. How did they manage to take it in through the much smaller doorway? They did not, really. They first installed the idol and then built the entire 66 m structure around it with utmost care! This was a bold step, because even a small accidental scratch on the idol during the construction would have rendered it unfit for worship and they would have had to start from scratch!

Now about those massive blocks of granite – how did they haul those without a crane? Scholars have a theory. The masons designed a ramp of tightly packed mud, which spiralled around the tower. As the tower grew, so did the ramp. Every day, without a break, a heavy load of granite was carved, hauled up the ramp and installed in place. After about seven years, when the top of the tower was completed, the engineers carefully demolished the ramp. The fact that it took all that weight and has stood there solidly makes the Big Temple an engineering marvel.

There's more. The gigantic granite blocks in the Big Temple are not held together by cement or any other binding agent! Each block was chiselled to perfection by stonemasons and was placed so snugly with the next block that the sheer weight of the stone simply locked the tower together. In all, Rajaraja used up to 130,000 tonnes of granite for the temple. And this humongous structure stands on a random rubble foundation that is only about 6-7 feet deep. This ancient technique uses uneven stones for the foundation and can handle soil shifts even during an earthquake. One thousand years and six earthquakes later, the *vimana* still stands majestically erect!

One persistent myth around the Big Temple is that the rounded cupola on the very top of the tower, called the *kalasam*, is a single piece of stone, which weighs, according to some estimates, about 80 tonnes. Did they roll it up to the top of the *vimana*? It took a team of experts to analyse the cupola and see for themselves that the big round stone was actually made up of segments, a bit like those of an orange. They had been carved separately, and then fitted together so cleverly that it seemed like one large stone.

The proud Rajaraja named the temple Rajarajeswaram after himself, so that the temple would keep his memory alive. However, the mighty Cholas were vanquished in 1279 CE. Later dynasties that ruled over Thanjavur lovingly maintained and added to the temple.

But sadly, the names Rajarajeswaram and Rajaraja were consigned to oblivion and everyone just called it

How did this myth come about and why is it so strong? A clue comes from another folk story. It says that Rajaraja was inspecting the site just before the consecration. It was the tallest tower then, and he wanted an assurance from his architect, a man named Kunjara Mallan Rajaraja Raman Perunthachan. 'What if such a tall structure collapsed?' he is said to have asked. Raman replied with supreme confidence: 'Your Majesty, not even its shadow will fall down!' And the myth caught on that its shadow would never fall on earth. The truth is that the tower stands tall and it casts a long shadow, without a shadow of doubt!

Rajaraja Chola built the Brihadeeswara Temple in 1010 CE. But the structure we see today has the imprint of many different dynasties that ruled over Thanjavur over the next 800 years. By the mid-13th century, the Pandyas defeated the Cholas. And during their brief rule, the Pandyas too made their contributions; the Periyanaki Amman shrine is believed to be their addition. By the late 14th century, Thanjavur fell to the Vijayanagara Empire, which lasted for more than 150 years. They appointed viceroys called Nayaks to rule over Thanjavur, and by the mid-16th century, the Nayaks declared themselves independent rulers of Thanjavur. After them came the Marathas who defeated the Nayaks in the late 17th century. They ruled for nearly 200 years until the mid-19th century. The Pandyas, the Vijayanagara kings, the Nayaks and the Marathas were all very generous patrons of this temple. Even today, one of the trustees of the temple management committee is a direct descendant of the Maratha kings.

the Big Temple or Periya Kovil, simply by virtue of its size. And so it was, until October 1887, when Hultzsch and Venkayya deciphered previously unread inscriptions in the temple.

Then, in 1931, came another pleasant surprise. There were always rumours of secret passages inside the temple, but no one had found any. That year, a history professor, S.K. Govindaswamy, was working on a hunch that the

When Hultzsch and Venkayya decoded the Big Temple inscriptions, they unearthed a treasure trove of information. The inscriptions give an incredible insight into the Chola style of administration and the society of those times. They give a full inventory of all the bronze idols and the priceless jewellery that the royal family had donated to the temple. Sadly, today, only two of those bronze figurines and none of the jewellery remain. The inscriptions also include a list of employees, their duties, remuneration and punishments. The list of employees is long: sweepers, lamp lighters, torchbearers, cooks, flag bearers, singers, dancers, priests and even an astronomer for calculating the right date and time for rites and festivities. The temple was well funded, and there were rules for managing the surplus wealth: how it may be invested and to whom money could be lent and at what rates of interest. The temple was expected to feed devotees and the poor. The inscriptions even had recipes for the dishes to be cooked!

Cholas, who had created such beautiful sculptures, must have left great paintings behind as well. His investigations led him to a dark and narrow passage around the inner sanctum. This secret corridor was covered with beautiful paintings dating to the 18th century when the temple was under the control of the Marathas.

One day, as the professor was examining these paintings, miraculously a piece of plaster from the wall fell down, revealing a tiny segment of an *older* painting behind it. That's when he realized that the Marathas had painted over 11th-century Chola murals. The panels were large and very beautifully rendered. It took several years of painstaking restoration to expose the older paintings that lay underneath without causing damage to them. Today, we can see neatly executed copies of these paintings in the temple museum. The original murals are sealed up in the secret passage to protect them.

More recently, many sculptures of Bharatanatyam dancing poses have been found. This told scholars how old the dance form is and that Rajaraja himself patronized it. Are there more surprises in the temple? Perhaps. But myths notwithstanding, the temple has certainly achieved its creator's purpose of telling the story of a remarkable emperor to future generations.

Murals are a special type of wall art. First, a coat of lime is applied on the wall. Then, within a short window of time – about 9-12 hours – the mural theme is quickly painted before the lime dries. Thus, the paintings get fixed permanently. The challenge for the officials of the Archaeological Survey of India was to carefully de-layer Maratha art to unravel Chola art. It took several years of delicate, painstaking effort.

28

The Cambodian King of Kanchipuram

VAIKUNTA PERUMAL TEMPLE, KANCHIPURAM

For over six hundred years, they ruled over
vast southern lands;
Arts and architecture flourished as the kingdom passed
through many able hands;
These legendary Pallava kings feature in many a local lore,
But the most successful of them all came from distant
South-East Asian shores.
The story is carved on sculptures that seem
oddly out of place
In one of the oldest Indian cities, inside a very sacred space.

Kanchipuram, a city near Chennai, is one of the oldest continuously inhabited cities in India. For centuries, it was the capital of powerful kings, and a seat of learning and religion. It is one of the 'Sapta-puris' or seven holy cities of the Hindus and was once called the 'city of a thousand temples'. Even today there are more than 100 temples there, many of them over 1,000 years old. That includes the famous Vaikunta Perumal Temple, built in

Vaikunta Perumal Temple

the late eighth century CE. This temple is worshipped as a 'Divya Desam' or one of the 108 most sacred shrines for Lord Vishnu.

What makes this temple unique, from a historical standpoint, is a series of sculpted panels on the inner walls of the temple. Some of these depict the political history of the region and offer a rare glimpse into events that transpired nearly 1,300 years ago. They narrate stories of the Pallava dynasty, their legendary origins and the battles they fought. Among these ancient wall panels are some depictions of people with unmistakably oriental features. They might seem oddly out of place in one of the holiest shrines for Lord Vishnu, until you consider the history of the region. These sculptures could very well be pointing to the Cambodian heritage of the Pallavas! This is the story of a prince from Cambodia-Vietnam, who saved the Pallava dynasty from extinction.

The Pallavas were a powerful dynasty who ruled parts of present-day northern Tamil Nadu, southern Andhra Pradesh and Karnataka between the third and the ninth centuries. Between the sixth and the eighth centuries, at the peak of their power and glory, they were embroiled in a bitter struggle for supremacy with the Chalukyas, their neighbours who also rose to great heights at around the same time. The Chalukyas ruled over most of present-day Karnataka and parts of Maharashtra from their capital Vatapi (now Badami in Karnataka).

Initially, it seemed that the Pallavas had the upper hand. In the mid-sixth century, a Pallava king successfully invaded and destroyed the Chalukya capital, Vatapi, killing the Chalukya King, Pulakeshin II. But the tables turned nearly a century later, when a Chalukya prince avenged the defeat by capturing the Pallava capital, Kanchipuram. The Pallava king, Parameswara Varman II, had to surrender and pay a huge tribute. Eager to restore his honour, he regrouped and invaded Chalukya territory in 731 CE, only never to return. He was killed in battle.

Parameswara Varman had no children, and therefore there was no heir to lead the kingdom. The Pallava kingdom was plunged into a constitutional crisis. The nobles of the kingdom conferred to resolve it. After much thought, they came up with an unusual solution. They decided to bring home a descendant from another branch of the Pallava lineage – the kings of Kambojadesha, or present-day Cambodia and Vietnam.

But how did these distant South-East Asian lands have Pallava descendants?

The Pallavas had always maintained strong trade ties with the kingdoms in South-East Asia. About 140 years

Folklore in Cambodia has many legends of an Indian man marrying a local princess and creating a new race of people, centuries before Bhima Varman. In one story, sage Swayambhu Kambu reached ancient Cambodia and married a Naga Princess named Mera. The union of Kambu and Mera produced the Khmer (Ka + Mer) people of Kambu-ja land.

A Tamil prince sails to a land 2,600 km away that is entirely different in language, religion and culture; he marries a local princess and the local people accept him as king! It may sound like fiction, but it is an entirely plausible story. The fact is that these cultures were not as unalike as one might imagine. There is enough historical evidence to believe that when Bhima Varman landed in Kambojadesha, it was against the backdrop of centuries of intermingling between the local Funan people and Indians from the subcontinent's east coast. The local Kambojas were Hindus, who could speak and write Sanskrit, with remarkable exposure to Indian culture. Tamil ships had been sailing to South-East Asia and southern China even as far back as the Sangam era (roughly between third century BCE and third century CE). During Pallava times, there were powerful Tamil merchant guilds that traded like multinational corporations in far-eastern countries. The ocean 'highway' from Pallava ports such as Mamallapuram to the various South-East Asian ports was like a maritime Silk Route. Cyclones and pirates made these journeys risky, but the guilds managed them well and earned profits.

before Parameswara Varman, a Pallava prince named Bhima Varman had migrated to Kambojadesha.

Bhima Varman was the younger brother of the then ruling Pallava king. In Kambojadesha, he married a local princess and got the opportunity to become an independent ruler there. His descendants still ruled Kambojadesha.

Cut back to 731 CE. The nobles in Kanchipuram calculated that if a prince from that family could be brought in to be crowned, it would be a happy homecoming for an expatriate Pallava prince, and Kanchipuram could still get a blue-blooded Pallava ruler! With this plan in mind, an empowered committee set sail for Kambojadesha. Meanwhile, the Pallava army braced itself for a Chalukya attack, which was imminent.

In Kambojadesha, the committee presented their credentials to King Kadavesa Hiranya Varman, who was Bhima Varman's descendant. The crown of Kanchipuram was offered to his sons. The first three sons declined. But the youngest prince, Parameswara Pallavamalla, barely 13 at that time, accepted the offer. The emissaries returned triumphantly with the young prince. He received a regal welcome at Kanchipuram and was crowned as King Nandi Varman II of the mighty Pallava dynasty.

But there was no time for celebrations. Very soon, the Chalukyas attacked in full force and captured Kanchipuram. Nandi Varman, who was a minor, was not permitted to engage in combat. The Pallavas were defeated, and the boy-king had to flee his kingdom. The victorious Chalukyas installed a puppet king named Chitramaya on the throne of Kanchipuram.

Nandi Varman, however, had not left a life of princely luxury back in Kambojadesha, only to become a royal refugee in India. He was made of sterner stuff, and fought back. In this, he had the unstinting support of the Kanchi citizens and of his trusted general, Udayachandran, a commander whose family had served the Pallava kings for generations.

Then, to tilt the scales in his favour, Nandi Varman very strategically married Reva, the daughter of the Rashtrakuta King, Dantidurga. The Rashtrakutas were kings from the Gulbarga region of Karnataka. They were originally feudatories of the Chalukyas, but they aspired for independence. With this marital alliance, Nandi Varman was assured of military support from the Rashtrakutas against their common enemy, the Chalukyas. Within a few years, their combined forces successfully defeated Chitramaya, and the Chalukyas were driven out of Kanchipuram.

Nandi Varman now began consolidating his position. He engaged in battles with the neighbouring Chera and Pandya kingdoms, and secured the southern and western borders. By 750 CE, the Pallava kingdom was restored to its former size and glory. The teenage prince from Kambojadesha had grown into a mighty ruler of a vast Pallava kingdom.

Now that political stability was established, Nandi Varman focussed his attention on art, architecture and literature. Being an accomplished Tamil and Sanskrit scholar himself, he encouraged traditional performing arts like 'Chakyar Koothu' and 'Koodiyattam'. Although Nandi Varman was a staunch Vaishnavite, he was tolerant of other faiths as well. During his reign, temple architecture blossomed again, and the Muktesvara Temple and Vaikunta Perumal Temple in Kanchipuram were his projects.

Nandi Varman went on to rule for 63 years, making him the longest reigning Pallava king. Thanks to his

How do we know so much about the Pallava kings? For one, the Pallavas created artistic – and, eventually, very informative – panels like the one in Vaikunta Perumal Temple. Many of these are pictorial representations of events. They also carved inscriptions on stone, like the ones you can see in the same temple. Which language did they write in? The early inscriptions were written in Sanskrit or Prakrit, and in later years Tamil became more prevalent. Sometimes, the same messages were written in different scripts. The Atiranachanda cave inscriptions in Mamallapuram are in Sanskrit, but written in both Nagari and Pallava Grantha scripts. The Pallavas also left a number of government records engraved on copper plates. The Maidavolu plates were created circa 305 CE by the Pallava King Sivaskanda Varman. This is thought to be one of the oldest copper plate inscriptions in India.

We also have written evidence about the Pallavas from writings by others. Thirumangai Alwar, the Vaishnavite poet-saint has written several verses extolling the greatness of Nandi Varman. Chinese visitor Xuanzang travelled in India during 629–645 CE. His travelogues tell us a lot about the achievements of the Pallavas. He recorded that Pallava King Narasimha Varman sent envoys to the Chinese emperor. Many kingdoms in Cambodia and Indonesia had rulers with surnames like Varman – a typical Pallava royal title. And there are mentions of Pallavas in many inscriptions in Cambodia – both in Sanskrit and Khmer languages.

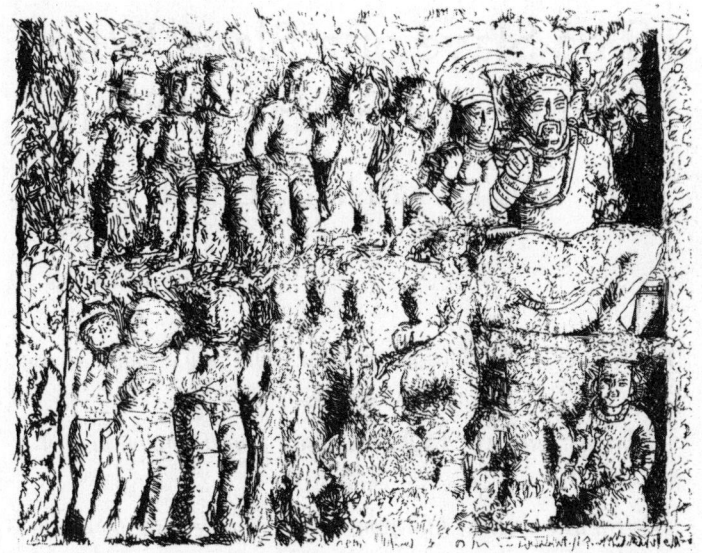

Temple wall panel depicting a man with unmistakably oriental features
(*top, extreme right*)

vigour, the rejuvenated Pallava dynasty went on to rule well into the late ninth century. They outlasted their rival Chalukyas by nearly 150 years. Quite an achievement for an immigrant boy who came from a land far away, don't you think? The beautiful panels on the walls of the Vaikunta Perumal Temple serve as a reminder of the Pallavas' South-East Asian connection.

29

The Slave of a Slave Who Became the Sultan of Delhi
QUTB MINAR, DELHI

His master was a slave at one time, who saw a dramatic rise to power –
The first sultan of Delhi who built a well-known victory tower;
This master bought him from a slave market and took him under his wing –
When the master died, this slave of a slave took over as the new king!

Most kings are born into royal families. And most inherit the crown merely by virtue of their birth; the eldest son of a king usually goes on to become the next king. There are exceptions, of course, and throughout history, there are any number of instances of nobles, ministers, generals and even commoners usurping the throne and starting their own royal line.

But what if you were born a slave? Could you still aspire to be king? Now, imagine the slave of a slave becoming a king!

Does that sound too far-fetched? Eight hundred years ago, Delhi was witness to both these events.

The breathtaking Qutb Minar in Delhi is the tallest brick tower in the world. This towering monument was started in 1192 by Qutb-ud-din Aibak, a former slave who became the king of Delhi. After his death, his slave, Iltutmish, took over the throne and carried forward the construction of Qutb Minar. He built the next three floors. Both these kings belonged to the Mamluk or Slave dynasty of Delhi, and this is their incredible story.

Qutb Minar

In the last years of the 12th century, the region that is Delhi today was ruled by a powerful Rajput ruler named Prithviraj Chauhan. He ruled over a large kingdom and had a strong army. At that time, in Afghanistan, a local king named Mu'izz-ud-din Muhammad Ghori was becoming powerful. And he was steadily advancing east – into India. He had conquered parts of north-west India, and Delhi was now within his reach. Back then, for invading kings from Central Asia, Delhi was an access point to the riches of the fertile Indo-Gangetic plains. And so, control of Delhi was always coveted. In 1191, he met Prithviraj Chauhan in the Battle at Tarain, about 150 km north of Delhi. Ghori's army was soundly defeated and he was badly wounded. Ghori fled, and Prithiviraj allowed him to flee, a tactical error that would cost him dearly. Just a year later, Ghori returned. And this time, at the Second Battle of Tarain, he won.

Prithviraj was captured and, by most accounts, he was executed. Ghori marched into Delhi and seized it easily. Then, he returned to his own country, leaving Delhi in charge of his trusted slave, Qutb-ud-din Aibak.

Qutb-ud-din Aibak was a Mamluk. Born to Turkic parents in 1150 CE, in a village in modern-day Kazakhstan, He was taken a slave and sold as a young boy. 'Mamluk' in Arabic, roughly translates to 'slave' or more precisely 'an owned person'. The Mamluk system of Asia was a marginally more humane version of slavery than the one commonly practised in the West. Mamluks were sold and bought in the market, but they were nurtured as valuable investments. They were educated, trained and given responsible assignments. Turkic slaves from the Eurasian steppe lands were highly prized as warriors. Often, they were trained in martial arts and deployed in the owner's army. They got promoted according to their competence, and could achieve a high social status. Occasionally, if a Mamluk suitably impressed his master, he could receive 'manumission', which meant a release from bondage, to become a free citizen. A Mamluk's life was tough, but not degrading or hopeless.

Qutb-ud-din's first master treated him well and educated him in both martial arts and religious studies. When the master died, Aibak was put up for sale again. As luck would have it, he was purchased by the king of the land, Sultan Muhammad of Ghor, also known as Muhammad Ghori. Muhammed soon spotted Aibak's talent and, under his watchful eye, Aibak rose to become a trusted army commander.

In the momentous Second Battle of Tarain, when Ghori attacked and captured Delhi, Aibak stayed close to Ghori and guarded him through the battle. After Delhi was taken, Aibak supported Ghori in quashing rebellions and consolidating territories. Increasingly, Ghori relied more on his Mamluk generals than even his own clansmen. He especially trusted Aibak, looking upon him as a son. Before he returned to Afghanistan in 1206, Ghori appointed Aibak as his viceroy in Delhi.

Ghori was mysteriously assassinated on his way to Afghanistan, and suddenly Aibak was left without a mentor. The other generals tried to grab control of Ghori's Indian territories. But Aibak handled the volatile situation competently and managed to hold on to the reins through a clever mix of diplomacy and force. Technically, he was still a slave. So when Ghori's nephew, Ghiyas-ud-din Mahmud, became the new king of Ghor, Aibak applied for manumission from him.

Ghiyas-ud-din granted him the manumission and also recognized him as the ruler of Hindustan. With that, Aibak became the first sultan of the Delhi Sultanate, and the first king of the Mamluk dynasty.

Aibak ruled for a mere four years. His end was as dramatic as his rise to power. The story goes that, one day, Aibak was playing a game of *chogan*, a kind of polo popular in those days. His horse stumbled, Aibak was thrown off, and the horse fell over him. He died instantly.

With no appointed successor, a power struggle immediately ensued in the Delhi Sultanate. In the chaos that followed, a man named Iltutmish edged out all the other rivals and took over as the king of Delhi. Shams-ud-din Iltutmish happened to be Aibak's favourite slave, and his story is uncannily similar to Aibak's.

Iltutmish was born a chieftain's son. But when he was still quite young, his jealous brothers sold him to a slave dealer. A few years later, as a strapping young man, he was brought to the Ghazni market for sale. There, he caught the eye of Qutb-ud-din Aibak, then a powerful slave commander under Muhammad of Ghor. With his permission, Aibak purchased Iltutmish.

Iltutmish was now a slave of a slave. But Aibak treated him like a son and under his mentorship, Iltutmish rose to become a successful military commander. Just like Aibak, he too was ambitious enough to work his way to the top. In time, he even married Aibak's daughter. When Aibak became the ruler of Delhi, Iltutmish was appointed governor of a province named Badaun. And after Aibak died, Iltutmish took over as the Sultan of Delhi.

Many scholars consider Iltutmish to be the real founder of the Delhi Sultanate. It was he who shifted the capital of the sultanate from Lahore to Delhi. He went on to rule for 25 long years. His greatest legacy is his contribution to architecture. In 1192 CE, Aibak started building the Qutb Minar, a monument to mark the victory of his master, Muhammad of Ghor, in Delhi. But by the time Aibak died, only the ground floor had been built. Iltutmish built the next three storeys.

More importantly, Iltutmish revolutionized architectural style in India. He brought in artisans from

At 73 m, the Qutb Minar is said to be the world's tallest brick tower. Who built this tower? That depends on which floor you are looking at. Qutb-ud-din Aibak started the building of the tower, and completed the ground floor and Iltutmish, added the next three storeys. In 1369, the tower was struck by lightning and the top storey was damaged. So the sultan of the time, Firuz Shah Tughlaq, repaired the structure and added one more storey and a cupola, making it a five-storeyed tower. Lightning struck a second time in 1505. This time, Sikandar Lodi, who ruled over Delhi then, repaired the damage. In 1540, another ruler, Sher Shah Suri, added a new entrance to the monument. How do we know all this? The inscriptions on the minar give us an almost complete history of the tower with the names of all the kings who contributed to it.

Inscriptions on Qutb Minar

Persia to work with local craftsmen. The resulting fusion was called Indo-Islamic architecture, which defined the Indian architectural landscape for several centuries. You can see the tomb of Iltutmish within the Qutb Minar complex, with many styles of Islamic calligraphy sitting pretty amid lotuses, diamonds and other local motifs.

The Second Battle of Tarain was a decisive turning point in Indian history. It brought in Turkic Muslim rulers to India, who, unlike the earlier invaders, did not just plunder and retreat, but stayed back and made India their home. Although the Mamluk dynasty ended by 1290 CE, Delhi would be ruled by Muslim kings for nearly 700 years after this. And it all began with a slave, and then the slave of a slave who became the sultan of Delhi. The majestic Qutb Minar still stands tall as a testament to the perseverance and ambition of these slaves-turned-kings.

30

The Curse on the Mysore Maharajas

MYSORE PALACE, MYSURU

A royal family that for centuries was popular and strong,
Was haunted by a curse of one who felt wronged;
Their majestic palace, a symbol of their might and glory
Houses an old shrine inside that tells this poignant story.

The Mysore Palace, also known as the Amba Vilas Palace, is a very popular tourist attraction in Mysuru, India. Its beautiful interiors are sumptuously decorated in teak, sandalwood, ivory and silver, with many precious artefacts on display. Most parts of the palace are open to the public, but one portion continues to be the private residence of the Wodeyar (or Wadiyar) royal family.

The Wodeyar dynasty ruled Mysore state for nearly six centuries, and over this period, they brought about several developments, cultural and social, that were far ahead of their time. Though they no longer rule the kingdom, the Wodeyars still remain an inseparable part of the region's culture. They command a lot of respect from the local population even decades after the princely state of Mysore joined the Indian Union.

When the previous palace was burnt down in a fire accident in 1897, a new palace was commissioned. It was designed by the famous British architect, Henry Irwin, in the Indo-Saracenic style. Irwin fused the finest elements of Indian and western architecture: sculpted pillars, ornate ceilings, Islamic domes, stained glass windows, glazed tiles and Czechoslovakian chandeliers, all capped with a five-story tower. Other attractions include paintings by Raja Ravi Varma (a renowned painter who belonged to the Travancore royal family) and a pavilion showcasing an eclectic collection of dolls from the 19th and 20th century. Among other structures, the palace complex has the residential quarters of the royal family and two durbar halls. During Dussehra and other holidays, the palace is brilliantly lit up with nearly 100,000 lamps.

In the 600 years of Wodeyar rule, the Mysore Palace was built, destroyed, rebuilt and remodelled many times. The palace complex has many structures including Hindu temples. One shrine where the erstwhile royal family prays even today, is dedicated to Alamelamma, the former queen and widow of Tirumala, the last viceroy of the Vijayanagara Empire. This shrine plays an important role in the grand Dussehra celebrations in Mysuru even now. During the nine–day Navaratri festival, the heads of the Wodeyar family are mandated to stay within the palace and are only free to move around on the ninth evening after offering prayers at the Alamelamma shrine.

But why would the royal family of Mysore build a shrine to the widow of a former Vijayanagara viceroy?

Mysore Palace

And why would they continue to revere it even now?

Legend has it that this shrine is associated with a long-standing curse that is believed to have haunted the Wodeyar family for centuries. It is said to be the result of an event that occurred in the early 17th century.

During the 14th and 15th centuries, before the Wodeyar dynasty ruled these parts, the Vijayanagara Empire ruled almost all of south India and was one of the most powerful regimes in India at the time. Its capital was Hampi, in present-day Karnataka, and Mysore was a province of this empire. In 1399, King Harihara II of Vijayanagara appointed Yaduraya, a local chief, as the overlord of the Mysore kingdom. The word Wodeyar means 'lordship' in Kannada. And from then on, the Wodeyars ruled as feudatory kings of Mysore under the Vijayanagara banner.

However, by the mid-16th century, the Vijayanagara Empire had started weakening. In 1565, the then Mysore king, Timmaraja Wodeyar II, saw an opportunity to break free from the empire and declared Mysore an autonomous kingdom. Mysore still nominally acknowledged the Vijayanagara emperor, but was independent for all practical purposes. The enterprising Wodeyar kings began expanding their lands by annexing the territories of their neighbouring kingdoms in Karnataka and Tamil Nadu.

By the 17th century, the once mighty Vijayanagara Empire had become a mere shadow of its earlier glorious self. It was during this time that Raja Wodeyar of Mysore set out to capture the neighbouring territory of Srirangapatna, one of the few territories still under the control of Vijayanagara. After capturing the Srirangapatna Fort, Raja Wodeyar dethroned the then ruler Tirumala, a viceroy of the Vijayanagara Empire. After this defeat, Tirumala, along with his two wives, quietly retired to a town named Talakad (now Talakadu). One of the wives, Alamelamma, was a staunch devotee of Goddess Ranganayaki of the Srirangapatna Temple. She owned a large collection of exquisite jewels and, as an act of devotion, she took great pleasure in adorning the goddess with her jewels, particularly with a beautiful pearl nose-ring from her exquisite jewellery collection. When she retired to Talakad with her husband, she naturally took all her jewels with her.

Shortly thereafter, Tirumala died and Alamelamma moved to a nearby village called Malangi. Meanwhile, Raja Wodeyar had heard about Alamelamma's priceless jewellery. He sent a messenger to Malangi, demanding that Alamelamma hand over her jewels to the king. He reasoned that since her husband had been defeated in a fair battle, the jewels rightfully belonged to him. Alamelamma sent the pearl nose-ring but not the rest of her jewel collection. The miffed raja sent his soldiers back with orders to confiscate all her jewels. Forced to yield her personal treasures that she held so dear, Alamelamma jumped into the River Kaveri and ended her life, but not before pronouncing a curse on the Wodeyars:

'May Talakad turn into a barren expanse of sand. May the River Kaveri in Malangi turn into a dangerous whirlpool. And may the Wodeyars never have any children.'

According to folklore, Alamelamma was so devout that her curse became a divine pronouncement. Deeply upset by the curse, the repentant Raja Wodeyar immediately built a shrine for Alamelamma inside the palace, installed her statue in it and worshipped it sincerely.

However, the curse stuck and mysterious things began to happen in Mysore after this incident. Talakad town, once a historic temple city, slowly got submerged under several metres of sand. The south-west monsoon shifted sands at the rate of nine to ten feet every year and several temples have been completely buried under the sand. Archaeologists are still digging them up.

That was not all. Just as her curse predicted, the River Kaveri, which flows near Malangi village, is considered unsafe for swimming, because of its dangerous whirlpools. The river takes a sharp turn at Malangi and that could be causing whirlpools and currents. Scientists attribute it to a geological fault that could have shifted the course of the River Kaveri at Malangi. But the legend of the curse makes a more compelling story and is more widely used to explain away these unusual phenomena.

There was more. The Wodeyar family started being haunted by a strange tragedy. Since the 17th century, every alternate Wodeyar king has been childless and has

The interiors of the Mysore Palace

had to adopt a close relative to continue the dynasty. In 1610, Raja Wodeyar's only surviving son died on the eve of the Dussehra festival. Between 1617 and 1704, four rulers of the Wodeyar clan did not have natural heirs and had to adopt from close relatives to continue the dynasty. There was some relief when Kanteerava Narasaraja, a natural heir, became king in 1704. Sadly, he was born deaf. The last natural-born heir died in 1732 and the Yaduraya lineage ended. Between 1732 and 1796, five kings came to power. And, every time, a natural-born heir to the throne would remain childless, while an adopted son who became the next king would beget an heir. This unusual phenomenon seemed to follow a pattern!

Despite the so-called curse, the kingdom of Mysore continued to flourish. Raja Wodeyar continued expanding and strengthening his kingdom after the fall of the Vijayanagara kingdom. When he handed over the throne to his successor, Mysore had become one of the richest and strongest kingdoms on the subcontinent. Between 1761 and 1799, the Wodeyars came to be controlled by two army generals of Mysore, Hyder Ali and his son, Tipu Sultan.

Although Tipu Sultan never lived in the palace complex, he remodelled it. He demolished some old structures, built new fortifications within the complex and renamed it his capital city of Nazarabad. The temples within the complex were left untouched. Tipu Sultan fought against the British and was finally defeated and killed by them in the Fourth Anglo-Mysore War in 1799. The British now took control of the large and prosperous Mysore state. They reinstalled the Wodeyar kings back on the throne of Mysore, but as vassal kings. The British held all the power now, but the Wodeyar kings continued to rule the princely state of Mysore until Indian independence when the kingdom of Mysore was merged with the Indian Union and the Wodeyars lost all political power.

Through all this, and even after ceding their kingdom to the Indian Republic, the Wodeyars apparently continued to be haunted by Alamelamma's curse.

In 1947, after India became independent, the kingdom of Mysore merged with India. Most of its royal wealth was taken over by the government of India. The Wodeyars continue to live in the Mysore Palace, retain a certain ceremonial lifestyle, and are respected by the people of Mysuru as the 'Royal Family'. The titular king still presides over the famous ten-day holy festival of Dussehra, which is celebrated grandly. He graces many social and religious functions in this capacity.

Jayachamaraja Wodeyar (r. 1940-74) was an adopted son. His natural son Srikanta Datta Narasimha Wodeyar, the titular king (1974-2013), who inherited the title, was childless. Therefore, he adopted his grand-nephew, Yaduveer Krishna Datta Wodeyar. Yaduveer became the titular king in 2015. Predictably, a son and heir was born to him in 2016. The royal family worships Alamelamma even now, in the hope that one day, she might be moved to withdraw her 'curse'.

Acknowledgements

This book credits a handful of authors who have worked tirelessly to give this collection of stories a compact form. But these stories have truly been a labour of love for all of us at Storytrails. I am grateful to all those who have been a part of our journey over the last 15 years and have helped shape the ideas in this book in different ways.

Many stories in this book were inspired by questions from guests we have hosted on our walking tours over the years. I'd like to extend my thanks to all our tour leaders – our storytellers and researchers – whose untiring legwork has given us nuggets of first-hand information and fascinating trivia from the ground. A big shout out goes to Lakshmi Shankar, our head of operations, who has done this religiously in every city we operate in.

A special thanks to the Tamil Nadu Archaeology department and the Egmore Museum for helping us with access to excavation sites and the artefacts at the museums. I would also like to express my gratitude to many other historians and subject experts who were generous with their time and have added immensely to our understanding of different subjects covered in this book. They include (the late) Mr Muthiah, Dr Rajan, Dr Amarnath, Dr Chitra Madhavan, Mr Madhusudhanan Kalaichelvan, Mr Sharat Sundar Rajeev, Dr Swapna Liddle, Ms Rana Safvi, Dr Alamelu Nachiappan, Prof. Vedachalam and Mr Ashok Panda. However, all views expressed in this book are our own and these experts bear no responsibility for any inaccuracies that may have crept into our telling of these stories.

Lastly, none of this would have been possible without the wonderful support of our editors at Hachette India. Thanks to Nimmy Chacko who seeded this idea and made this book a reality, and our fabulous editor Vatsala Kaul Banerjee, who very patiently guided us through the rules and conventions of the publishing world.

– Vijay Prabhat Kamalakara, Founder and CEO, Storytrails